Gypsy Girl

Gypsy Girl

Rosie McKinley

**HODDER &
STOUGHTON**

Publisher's Note

Rosie McKinley is a pseudonym. All names and other identifying
details have been changed to protect the privacy of Rosie's family.
Some characters are not based on any one person but are composite characters.

First published in Great Britain in 2011 by Hodder & Stoughton
An Hachette UK company

1

Copyright © Rosie McKinley 2011

The right of Rosie McKinley to be identified as the Author of the Work has been
asserted by her in accordance with the Copyright, Designs and Patents Act 1988.

A CIP catalogue record for this title is available from the British Library.

Hardback ISBN 978 1 444 70931 5
Trade Paperback ISBN 978 1 444 70867 7
eBook ISBN 978 1 444 7093 2

Typeset in Sabon MT by Hewer Text UK Ltd, Edinburgh

Printed and bound in the UK by CPI Mackays, Chatham ME5 8TD

Hodder & Stoughton policy is to use papers that are natural, renewable
and recyclable products and made from wood grown in sustainable forests.
The logging and manufacturing processes are expected to conform to the
environmental regulations of the country of origin.

Hodder & Stoughton Ltd
338 Euston Road
London NW1 3BH

www.hodder.co.uk

For my children, Sarah-Jane, Tyrone, Finn, Grace and Hope

Contents

I

Born on the Streets

I was born on a pavement. No, really, I was.

And it wasn't one of those pavements paved with gold either, like in the fairytales. No, this one was on the north side of Leeds on a drizzly Tuesday morning in February 1970, so my birthplace was paved with fag ends, blotches of discarded chewing gum and bird mess stains. Mammy had been stood by the side of the road desperately waiting for Daddy to come back and take her to the hospital. But I beat him to it and made my entrance there and then with no one around to witness Mammy give birth except a couple of snotty-nosed kids from one of the other caravans on our site.

'You never could do things properly,' Mammy would grumble as I was growing up. 'I was mortified sitting there in a pool of blood and God knows what,' she went on. 'Just because you decided it was time to make an appearance.'

She was right. I never did do things quite properly. Not the way Mammy and Daddy and the rest of our community might have wanted. I loved being a traveller and mostly I loved our traditional way of life. But from an early age I also had a strong sense that I wanted my life to be different.

'This don't seem right,' I'd think to myself as me and Mammy wrang out our towelling bedsheets with red, chapped hands on ice cold winter mornings while Daddy and my brother Kevin sat in the front of their truck supping mugs of mahogany-brown tea. But it was the only life I had ever known. And as far back as my brain could imagine, in our family, it had always been like this. We were all travellers, or gypsies, as everyone else in the world called us.

While most settled people have a family tree that looks pretty much like, well, a tree, in my family it looks more like the root system of some exotic plant. Cousins have married cousins, brothers and sisters have brought up their siblings and everyone is pretty much related to everyone else if you go back far enough.

My mammy's mother, Granny Mary O'Hara, had 18 children without breaking into a sweat. She was a short, chubby woman with large, strong hands. She could cook a full dinner for 20 over an open fire or pull the family trailer out of a muddy field while holding a baby under her arm. And she never got flustered. She came from a culture within our traveller community that boasted the best music makers and fiddlers. One of her brothers had even made a record and he was known as the fastest fiddler in southern Ireland.

Granny O'Hara loved sitting at night with the family while one of her brothers played 'Bonnie Kate' on his fiddle. Her feet would be tapping away while she managed to darn a pair of men's trousers in perfect time with the music. But she rarely sang herself. In fact, Granny – or Ol'Mammy as we called her – rarely spoke. She was too busy cooking, scrubbing and popping out kids at a rate of about one a year to sit around yacking.

It was Grandad – or Ol'Daddy – who had all the chat. He was the size of a giant, about 15ft tall with shoes like small boats and arms that constantly threatened to burst out of his shirtsleeves. (OK, maybe he wasn't entirely 15ft tall, but that was certainly how it seemed to me back then!) He was fearsomely strong and as fit as a teenager even though when I was growing up he was well into his forties. In the evenings if he went to the pub he'd race some of the other fellas home, except they'd be in their trucks or cars and he'd be running! He'd burst sweating and breathless back onto the site and it'd often be a good couple of minutes before the first truck screeched into the yard behind him.

Ol'Daddy was incredibly well respected and just knowing that would make my chest puff out with pride.

He'd been born in Ireland but travelled over to England in search of work in the early 1950s and stayed ever since. He was a good man and fair. If other travellers were in disputes with each other they'd come to him and he'd listen to all the sides then try to work out some agreement that everyone was happy with.

And he was a great parent and grandparent too. After supper he'd sit us on his lap until he ran out of knee space and the rest of the kids had to crouch around him, then he'd tell stories about ghosts and mermaids and giants that threw boulders across the Irish Sea. When it got to the really scary bit of the story, Ol'Daddy would fix me in his gaze as if I was the only kiddie there in the room. I always felt I was his favourite. He adored Mammy and I guess I must have reminded him of her when she was little. There was nowhere I'd rather be than sitting on Ol'Daddy's lap listening to his stories. And to tell the truth there were times when I wasn't even listening, just being close to him was enough for me. In Ol'Daddy's trailer the little'uns were always in bed before dark with their faces scrubbed and their prayers said. And if he and the other men were sat out by the fire chatting, Ol'Daddy would be the one who would come in regularly to check the kids were safe and sleeping soundly.

During the day Ol'Daddy was a scrap metal man. He drove around the streets looking for old iron railings, fireplaces or fridges that he would sell on, making a few pounds along the way.

My Mammy was her parents' first child and she was the apple of Ol'Daddy's eye. Throughout my childhood I always knew there was a special relationship between Mammy and Ol'Daddy. Around the fire in the evenings they'd banter and joke with each other and my Mammy's face lit up whenever he was around. Even when she married Daddy there was no way that they would move away from Ol'Mammy and Ol'Daddy and so my grandparents played a huge part in my childhood.

I was my parents' third child. When I turned up that morning on the pavement they'd already got Kevin, who was four and Bridget, who was two. Kevin was the typical doting brother, feeding me jelly babies when I was still just two days old! Bridget was my constant playmate or arch-enemy (depending on how we were feeling).

A couple of minutes after I made my sudden entrance into the world, surrounded by empty crisp packets and beer cans, Daddy turned up in an ambulance and carted me and Mammy off to hospital to be checked out by the doctors. Rather than think it was a pretty grim way to start life, Mammy was already convinced I was going to be a lucky child. I'd been born with what travellers call Our Lady's Veil over my face. This is when the baby is delivered with the amniotic sac, or caul, covering her face like a mask. In our culture it is a sign of good luck and means that the child is destined for great things or might have psychic powers. Sailors think keeping a caul can even stop them from drowning. Mammy and Daddy were delighted their baby had been born with such a lucky talisman. Mammy gently lifted the veil off my face and kept it safe in an old shoe box in the corner of our trailer. A couple of months later when a woman on our site gave birth to a terribly poorly baby, Mammy gave her my veil and the lady laid it onto her child's face. Apparently it saved the baby's life.

Within a couple of weeks of my birth we were on the move again and we set off in our caravan to a site west of Manchester. There was never any particular reason why we moved on, it was just what we did.

I was about eight months old, a chubby wee thing with tufts of coal-black hair sticking up like desert grass, when everything changed. I was just at that baby stage of sitting upright on my own for short periods before plunging forwards, headfirst into the ground. Mammy had put me in a playpen outside the front of our caravan and I was sat there happily bashing a multi-coloured plastic telephone while she got on with cleaning up the trailer. Daddy was out working with all the other men from the site. Suddenly there was all sorts of commotion around the place.

'Quick, Theresa, come quick,' someone shouted to Mammy. 'Patsy's real sick. She's been hit by a bus down the road.'

Patsy was my Mammy's younger sister. She was even skinnier and more glamorous than Mammy, with layered blonde hair like Farrah Fawcett and lips that were constantly cerise pink. She'd left the site that morning to go down the town for some shopping but had been hit by a bus as she crossed the road on her way back.

'She's bleeding, ring an ambulance,' people were shouting.

All around the site women were screaming and any men that were too old, ill or just plain lazy to have gone out to work, rallied themselves to help. There were about 40 people on that site and all of them were related to Auntie Patsy in some way.

Suddenly everyone had gone, running off down the road and leaving the site empty apart from me, still in my playpen, grinding the toy phone into the mud. It must have been then, with no one else around to occupy it, that a Rottweiler belonging to a family in another of the trailers became interested in me.

There were always ragged-looking dogs skulking around our site, sniffing out food or barking at strangers. The fiercest ones were sometimes tied up to their owners' trailers with lengths of string, but most of them just roamed free, wherever they fancied.

Maybe I cried out or tried to grab the dog. I really don't know as I was far too young to remember. But the story I was brought up with was that suddenly, with all the adults gone, the Rottweiler leapt into my playpen and clamped its jaws around my tiny throat.

Its teeth bit into my face and neck and blood spurted all over my pink gingham babygro.

The Rottweiler's jaw was so strong that it easily crushed my airways and when one of our neighbours returned to the trailers she found me barely able to breathe and soaked in blood.

Poor Mammy was called back immediately in a state of total shock. 'My baby, my baby,' she screamed as she picked up my virtually lifeless body. Her sister was so badly broke up in the smash that she was feared dead and now here was her new baby fighting for her life too.

Someone ran off to a payphone and called another ambulance and within minutes I was undergoing emergency surgery in the same hospital as Auntie Patsy.

I was in hospital for six months as they tried to rebuild my windpipe and treated the horrific bites on my face and neck. Every day Mammy would come up to visit me and bring me clean babygros and little toys, then go to visit Auntie Patsy who had head injuries and broken legs but miraculously made a full recovery. Slowly but surely I got better too. But the two incidents meant our family stayed for a while in Manchester as me and my aunt underwent treatment.

When I was allowed home I still struggled with swallowing and could choke very easily. All my food had to be liquidised or mashed and someone had to sit with me whenever I ate in case anything blocked my windpipe.

The dog attack upset Mammy real bad. I think she felt guilty she hadn't been able to protect me, but there was nothing she could have done. After that she started panicking that she couldn't look after me properly and she was constantly nervous that I was about to choke and she wouldn't be able to save me. So in the end she sent me to live in the trailer with Ol'Mammy and Ol'Daddy. That might sound strange to settled folk but it was quite normal in our culture for kids to go and live with other relatives for a while. And as we were all on the same site my Mammy and Daddy were only ever a couple of yards away anyway. But if I did start to choke at mealtimes, which most days I did, Ol'Daddy would just put his fingers down my throat, pick out whatever had got stuck, then let me carry on with my tea. The choking continued throughout my toddler years and right up to school age. Because of it, I wasn't allowed to eat meat but I loved it far too much to miss out. When no one was looking I'd nick meat off their plates then hide it under my mash. That was more like a proper dinner!

It wasn't hard to go round stealing food from other people's plates as mealtimes were mayhem. For most of the time I lived with Ol'Mammy and Ol'Daddy they had ten or eleven other kids at home as well as me. Because Mammy had been their eldest child some of the youngest were only a few years older than me. I never thought of them as uncles and aunts, they were playmates. Of Ol'Mammy's eighteen pregnancies, a couple of children were stillborn and some of the older ones had left home by the time I came along, but there was still always at least a dozen of us sitting down to eat at mealtimes.

Some of the time Ol'Daddy had two trailers and half of us would sleep in each. But at other times, if he'd sold one of the trailers, then we'd all bed down together. Ol'Daddy's trailer had two bedrooms, each with a double bed. Ol'Mammy and Ol'Daddy had one and the girls would lay down in the other, stretched out next to each other like matches in a box. The boys slept in the lounge area where the sofa cushions folded out to make another bed.

There wasn't much room and we'd never heard of the word 'privacy', but at least it was warm. Well, most of the time. As the youngest I spent a lot of nights shivering with cold because the bigger ones tugged the blankets off me and onto themselves. Or I'd find myself squeezed closer and closer to the trailer wall until I was barely able to breathe.

'Come on in here with us,' Ol'Daddy would say, throwing back the covers and pulling me up into bed between him and Ol'Mammy, when I appeared in their room, shaking with cold. To me, snuggled in between those two was the best place in the world. I quickly learnt that as the baby of the family with a wheezy chest and breathing problems, a few exaggerated coughs and splutters would always win me a place in the warmth of my grandparents' bed.

One night when I was about five, I was sharing the double bed with three of my aunties, Chrissie, Margaritta and Bernadette, and I messed the bed. They woke up to find themselves sharing my damp sheets. As you can guess, I wasn't the most popular at that moment, but being the baby I could still get away with anything. I had to be cleaned up though. It was the middle of the night and below freezing outside but it was the only place we had water. Chrissie, Margarita and Bernadette went out of the front door and pulled the tin bath out from its storage place under the trailer. I knew what was coming and I was already wriggling to get away from them.

Next they pulled out the farmers' milk churns where we

kept our water. Without a word of a lie, the ice on top was two inches thick. Margarita had to use a ladle to smash through it before she could pour out any water into the tub. Bernadette lifted me into the bath and sponged me down. It was so cold that at first I could barely breathe, let alone speak.

'No, please, don't,' I wailed.

'We've got to clean you up,' Bernadette hissed, trying not to wake up the whole site.

Within minutes I was back in the warmth of the caravan but my poor aunts were still outside washing and rinsing out the sheets. When they finally fell back into bed their hands were red raw and their bodies shook with cold.

In winter we would often wake up to find frost on the top blanket lying over us. With so many people breathing all night in such a small space the rooms were thick with condensation and the dampness just froze around us. Rivers of condensation would stream down the inside windows of the trailer leaving patches of damp on the windowsill all year round.

Ol'Daddy was always up early. By the time I padded out of the bed he would have turned on the gas heater to give us a little bit of warmth, been outside to wash his face in the ice-cold water and be well into a third cup of tea so strong that it left a permanent stain on the cup. The double-deck tape player in the kitchen would be blaring out tinny-sounding versions of traditional Irish folk tunes – all at half six in the morning.

Ol'Mammy was next up to get the fry on, filling the trailer with the delicious smell of bacon fat and eggs. Sometimes she'd make Coddle, a traditional travellers' meal which is sausages, bacon and potatoes in a kind of soup. It was just delicious. We'd all squash around the grey formica table in the middle of the trailer bolting down our breakfast before anyone else had a chance to snatch it from our plates.

When we were finished Ol'Daddy would give Ol'Mammy a kiss on the side of her head then go out and heave himself up into his lorry for another day on the search for scrap. Then us kids were shoved outside to wash our hands and faces in the steel milk churns with handles on the side that served as our personal wash basins. Ol'Daddy had picked up one each for us over the years and we made special marks on them to make sure they didn't get mixed up. Mammy's was always the easiest to spot because it shone like a mirror from her constant polishing.

The churns would be filled with rainwater or would have water poured into them from big plastic bottles that the men would bring home at night on the back of their trucks. They'd fill them up at petrol stations or stand-pipes at the side of the road. All the travelling men at that time had special keys that could open up any standpipe. And occasionally, friendly country people – which is what we called settled folk – would let us have water out of their taps.

From time to time Ol' Daddy would take one of his sons, Marty or Danny, with him to help him carry the scrap. And just occasionally, if I begged long enough and hard enough, I'd be able to go out with him on the lorry too. I'd have been about ten by then. I was a real tomboy and liked nothing better than messing around with trucks and lumps of metal. Dolls and toy teapots held no attraction for me at all. In Ol'Daddy's lorry I'd sit up the front, my legs sticking with sweat to the plastic seat, and look down on all the country people scurrying off to work or school. They were always in such a desperate hurry! I was so high up in that lorry that I felt like the Queen of England.

Sometimes as we jiggled along the roads, listening to Ol'Daddy's accordion music blaring out of the stereo, our eyes peeled for any old iron (literally!), I'd get a glimpse through a front window of a sitting room or a kitchen. I'd never been inside a house then, but everything looked pretty much the same as inside our trailer. There was the same brown draylon sofa in the front room and the same formica worktops in the kitchen. They were even covered in the same bottles of brown sauce and ketchup. Even the net curtains were the same as those in our trailer. But the big difference was that the only home I'd ever known had wheels and could move anywhere we wanted it to go.

'Why do country people always stay in one place?' I asked Ol'Daddy one day.

'They don't know how good it feels to be always moving on,' he said.

It was a good enough answer for me. As far back as I can remember, we were taught to treat country people with suspicion. 'They'll slag you off as soon as look at ya,' Ol'Daddy would say.

By the time Ol'Daddy got home from work, the fire would be on and Ol'Mammy would be cooking supper in the big black pots that hung over it. We had a two-ring hob inside the trailer too but Ol'Daddy preferred his food to be cooked outside. 'It tastes of the fresh air this way,' he would say. And he was right. It was delicious. It was incredible what meals Ol'Mammy could cook in those two pots over an open fire. There were stews and fry-ups and even Sunday roasts with the meat cooking away in one pot while the veg boiled in another.

It needed a hell of a lot of wood to keep that fire going. Me and my uncle Marty, who was five years older than me, and aunt Chrissie, who was four years older, spent hours tramping through woodlands near our site hunting for kindling to start the fire, twigs and branches to build it up, and logs to keep it roaring all night. We'd return to the site with just our legs sticking out from beneath the massive piles of wood we had collected. Then we'd have to lay it just the right way to make sure it took hold and didn't burn out after the first half an hour. But it seemed that no matter how much firewood we found, the next day Ol'Mammy would be at us again. 'Are you three going to hang around here all day or are you going to get off your backsides and fetch me some wood?'

Ol'Mammy made fresh bread every day with flour, buttermilk, a pinch of salt and baking soda. She'd roll it out on a tray then cook it on the hot coals of the fire. Ol'Daddy wouldn't eat bread from a shop; he said it tasted of nothing compared to Ol'Mammy's.

After tea would be when Ol'Daddy told us his stories. He couldn't read or write but he had an imagination that England's best writers couldn't compete with. Other times he'd get down on his knees and me and Chrissie would climb on top of him, slapping his backside as he pretended to be our old carthorse. He'd be laughing, always laughing and that made us laugh too.

Ol'Daddy spent hours in the evenings making horse-shoes from metal that he melted down in the fire then battered into shape. Then he'd fit them to his own horses or sell them at the travellers' fairs in the summer. And the men loved playing a game with the horseshoes that involved trying to throw them around a peg hammered into the ground 15 feet from where they were standing. They could spend hours chucking those horseshoes around, competing with each other, betting on who would win and squabbling over missed throws. On special occasions us kids were allowed to play too, but usually we weren't allowed to touch Ol' Daddy's horseshoes, they were far too precious.

There were always horses tied to stakes bashed into the ground around the edges of the site. Some of them were mangy-looking old things but I loved the ones with glossy chestnut coats and long swishing tails that swiped away the flies buzzing around them.

I was never allowed close to them, though, because after the Rottweiler attack I was diagnosed as asthmatic and horse hair made me wheezy.

'Keep away from that animal,' Ol'Mammy would yell if I ventured up to one of the horses, 'they'll play the devil with your chest.'

Ol'Daddy had a great eye for spotting a young horse that he'd be able to train up and sell on.

'This animal's wild,' men would say as they brought another bucking and braying horse round to our site to show Ol'Daddy.

He'd stand there frowning at it and shake his head. 'Aye, you're probably right, don't think I'll be able to do much with this'un,' he'd say before offering them a rock-bottom price. Two weeks later the pony would be eating out of Ol'Daddy's hand, trotting round the field and following commands like some kind of thoroughbred. I don't know how he did it. I guess the animals must have loved him and been happy to obey his commands. Whatever his technique, it worked. A year later Ol' Daddy would sell the horse on for twice what he'd paid for it. I'd be heartbroken when one of my favourite horses was sold but there'd soon be another one roaming around the site.

Come evening time, we'd know when bedtime was approaching the moment Ol'Mammy stoked the fire again to heat up water to fill the tin bathtub. Then we'd take it in turns to hop in for a rough scrub down with the flannel. I'm sure it would have been kinder to use sandpaper! Being near the end of the bathtub queue was bad news as you were left with cold, grimy water. And if you got in after Marty that was really, really bad. He was always filthy after a day running wild in the woods at the back of our site. When we were all clean Ol'Mammy would use the water to wash out our socks and knickers from the day then peg them up next to the fire. Everything stank of woodsmoke all the time. But even now I think it is the most comforting smell in the world.

2

A Girl Called Mud

Fires were lit for supper and the air would have turned damper by the time the men's lorries bounced back onto our site each evening.

A lot of the men were scrappers like Ol'Daddy and my Daddy. Others were labourers and some worked with tarmac, laying drives and mending potholes. They'd go house to house doing repairs and picking up work as they could find it. Some travellers had a bad reputation for charging over the odds for work but the fellas on our site were honest boys.

My favourite time was when the tarmac lorries returned home. I'd sneak out of our trailer then hide next to the trucks and breathe in deep lungfuls of the smell of warm tarmac.

I loved that smell, it was so rich and comforting. If no one was watching I'd push my pudgy little hands into any soft tarmac which had spilt down the back of the truck during the day's job. Then I'd peel off chunks of it and mould it in my hands before sticking my face right into it to breathe the smell in deeper.

I was probably only three or four when I took my strange fascination even further – and put some of the tarmac into my mouth and ate it. It tasted gloopy and I loved the sensation. That was it, my obsession had begun. From then on

I'd eat little lumps of tarmac every time I could pick warm chunks off the side of a lorry. People might think it sounds disgusting but it never once made me sick or gave me a tummy upset.

Then I started to eat mud, too. I'd sit on the patchy grass around the edge of the site and dig my fingernails into the ground, pull up a damp piece of earth and eat it. I could sit there chewing on the ground for hours on end. 'What the hell are you doing out there?' Ol'Mammy would call out to me. 'Will ya stop eating the ground like some kind of animal.'

And that was where I got my nickname – Mud. Except it wasn't just a nickname that people called me every now and again. As far as I was concerned, it *was* my name. I knew no other. 'What are you doing now, Mud,' Ol'Daddy would say. 'Do you want to play shops, Mud?' Bridget would say. 'Mud's just hit me,' Marty would yell. To every-one, I was Mud.

One spring afternoon when I was about seven and we were living near Liverpool, I went into town with my uncle and aunt, Marty and Chrissie. We went into one of the big department stores in the city centre and were racing around, laughing and joking on. Then I wandered into the ladies' perfume department and was instantly mesmerised by the glass cases full of delicate sparkling bottles and the exotic smells bursting from every counter. But when I looked round for Marty and Chrissie, they were gone. I was lost.

A lady with bright blue eyeshadow that twinkled when she blinked found me chewing my lip to stop the tears. I told her I was lost and she led me into a storeroom at the back of the shop, piled high with cardboard boxes. Ten minutes later

a policeman turned up. Ol'Daddy had always warned us to
beware of the police. Of all the country people who hated
travellers the police hated us most, he'd told us. But this
copper seemed kind. He had a strong Scouse accent and a
moustache so long that it tickled his teeth.

'So, what's your name then?' he asked, beaming down
at me.

'Mud,' I replied.

'Mud?' he said.

'Yes Sir, Mud.' We'd always been taught to be polite to
the police, whatever we might think of them.

'OK,' the policeman said, his moustache brushing his
teeth as he spoke. 'Mud what?'

I stared at him blankly.

'What's your surname, your second name?' he said.

'My name's Mud. Just Mud,' I repeated, feeling myself
about to start crying all over again.

'And have you any clue at all as to where you might live?'
he asked.

'With me Ol'Daddy,' I replied.

'Right. And where might that be?'

'In our trailer.'

It was a long process for the poor old copper but gradually he worked out that although I had no idea of my full
name, what our site was called, or the name of the road, I
did have a pretty good sense of direction. So he walked with
me out of the town centre and slowly but surely I was able
to lead us both back towards my home. We were almost
there when Ol'Daddy's lorry came juddering to a standstill
in the road next to us. Marty and Chrissie were side by side
on the front seat and I could tell by their white faces that

they'd been on the wrong end of a tongue lashing from Ol'Daddy about losing me.

Ol'Daddy jumped out of the cab, picked me up and held me up to his chest, which felt to me to be as broad and wide as a concrete paving slab.

'This little girl belongs to you then does she?' my moustachey policeman said to Ol'Daddy in a tone of voice he hadn't used earlier. Suddenly he seemed sneering and not so nice after all. But I realised then that Ol'Daddy was used to being spoken to like this.

'Yes, Sir,' he replied quietly, almost appearing to shrink and soften as he held me.

'Perhaps it might be worth teaching her what her proper name is then,' said the officer before turning and striding off back down the road.

When we got home, Ol'Daddy was steaming angry. Maybe he felt he'd been humiliated in front of his kids and granddaughter.

'From now on this child will be called by her proper name: Rosie,' he said.

So that was it. Mud had gone. I was now Rosie. Rosie McKinley.

Marty and Chrissie were my closest pals and partners in crime. I played with my sister Bridget a lot too but she was more of a girly girl. Bridget could spend hours lining up her Sindy dolls only to then rearrange them in a different order half an hour later. I preferred to be outside, riding my bike, tramping through the woods and getting dirty wherever and whenever possible.

Although they were my uncle and aunt, the age difference was so small that we were the best of mates. We did everything together. And most of those things were bad! With me being the youngest I was always a couple of yards behind the others and usually the first to get caught when we were up to no good. There'd be other kids from the sites who would muck about with us, but we were always the gang leaders. We never had time to sit indoors and complain about being bored and I never ever felt lonely. We were outside from first thing in the morning until Ol'Mammy's last scream of the day: 'Y'all get yourselves in here right now. It's time for bed.'

One of our favourite games was scavenging for old bricks and slabs of cement that we'd use to build our own houses at the edge of the site. The walls would wobble and fall over at the merest push but no one minded; it meant we could start building it all over again.

Marty and Chrissie were wild. Totally wild. They were always running into people's gardens in the houses near the site, jumping over fences and generally causing mischief. One of our favourite games was called Knockalash, which was like Knock Down Ginger. We'd take it in turns to knock on someone's door then run away before they answered it. It drove Marty and Chrissie mad that I couldn't run as fast as them and was always getting caught – because when the irate homeowner marched me back to Mammy it would be them that got a swipe round the ear for leading me astray.

There was one poor old lady at the end of a street near our site and we plagued her playing Knockalash. 'You keep away from her,' said Daddy. 'She cuts children up and eats them for her tea and if you go round there again she'll do it to you.' But of course to us kids, that threat just made creeping down her garden path all the more exciting. Maybe she really was like one of those witches in Ol'Daddy's stories. On the one hand, the thought terrified us, but on the other it was so exciting.

One evening I was babysitting for my younger brothers and sisters in Mammy and Daddy's trailer, but playing out with Marty and Chrissie at the same time. I was probably only about nine but that was thought perfectly old enough to babysit in our family. Every now and again I'd pop back into the trailer to check the little'uns were OK before nipping out again for another go of Knockalash. But somehow I managed to lock myself out of the trailer. Daddy would be mad if he found out I'd left the little'uns inside alone so I decided to break a window then get Marty to give me a leg up so I could reach in and undo the latch. My wrist was just through the broken glass when the child-eating woman from the house at the end of the road turned up at our trailer, frothing with anger. Marty and Chrissie were so terrified that they dropped me and my hand smashed down on the broken glass, slashing open my wrist. I was covered in blood and had a whole lot of explaining to do when Mammy got home.

The worst of it was that when the old lady saw the state of my arm she came rushing over and, rather than eat me up, she helped stop the bleeding by tying her scarf around the cut. She was actually a lovely woman and after that we became good friends. I'd fetch her fags from the corner shop when she'd run out then listen to her stories about those nice young American soldiers she'd met during the war.

Me, Marty and Chrissie would ride for miles around the

towns and countryside on our bikes. My Chopper bike was my pride and joy. I could do jumps and wheelies and skids on it better than any boy on the site. I had it for years and even when the saddle fell off and only one handlebar and one pedal worked and there was no rubber left on the wheels, I still couldn't bear to get rid of it. Daddy bought me a brand new shiny BMX for Christmas but I left it tied up by the side of the trailer and stuck to my Chopper instead, sitting sideways on the metal bar where the saddle had once been.

The three of us were a little gang and we didn't tell the grown-ups what we'd been up to, ever. It was our pact, even when things got out of hand, as they frequently did. One boiling hot summer afternoon we were staying near a canal in Liverpool and we went to play next to it. When we got there the lock gates were closed and the water was low. Marty and I were play-fighting and as it got more and more boisterous he shoved me and I went flying back into the water. And I couldn't swim. The water in the lock had started rising by then but I was still far too low down for anyone to be able to reach me. I kicked my arms and legs as hard as I could but my head kept slipping beneath the filthy water as it rose up all around me.

'Oh Jesus,' I prayed. 'Please don't let me drown.'

Chrissie was stood by the lock gates waving her arms around and yelling, 'Just do this and kick your legs.' Not that she could swim any better than me!

Marty ran off down the towpath and found a man cycling home from work.

'Please Sir, my niece, she's drowning, you've got to help.'

The fella pedalled his bike back towards me then jumped

straight into the filthy water and yanked me coughing and spluttering to the side. A couple of minutes later I was sat at the edge of the lock, safe but sopping wet, shaking with relief and punching Marty round the head as hard as I could manage.

My rescuer cycled off clearly furious he'd got himself sopping wet because of our fooling about. 'Bloody stupid kids,' we heard him yell as he disappeared off down the towpath. Marty felt terrible for ages afterwards and I never lost a chance to remind him about how he'd almost drowned me!

Another of our favourite games was climbing up onto the roofs of factories and houses then jumping from one to the other. Marty and Chrissie would always be up first and I'd be a couple of yards behind them, desperately trying not to wheeze or look like I couldn't do everything that they could do. One time in Manchester we even managed to climb underneath a bridge that stretched across a busy dual carriageway between two blocks of flats. A policeman saw us hanging 40 feet up in the air, pulled over in his car and started yelling at us to get down. But we were having far too much fun. And we could hardly stop once we were half-way across. If we'd fallen we'd have been killed instantly but we were too stupid back then to think of anything like that. Danger didn't bother us.

Then there was the time we got into real trouble. I was about 9 by then so Chrissie would have been 13 and Marty a year older. We were playing over at the park and a gang of country kids were winding the swings round and round the top bar so the seats got so high off the ground that no one else could use them. That always used to annoy me because it was awful when we went down the park with the little'uns and they couldn't play because some eedjit had thought it was hilarious to vandalise the swings.

'Look at those stupid kids over there,' I said to Marty, pointing out what they'd done. There were about eight of them and they were dead hard, with their shaved heads, mean pale faces and expensive white trainers nearly blinding me in the sunshine. But it didn't matter how tough they looked. Marty wasn't scared of anyone. Ol'Daddy used to say that he could be knocked over with a strong gust of wind but in his own mind he was built like Mohammad Ali.

'What the feck are you doin'?' he yelled across at the lads. Chrissie was stood squarely behind Marty. I was trying to sink into the ground behind both of them.

'Piss off, pikeys,' came the reply, quickly followed by a stone lobbed by one of the boys.

It wasn't like we'd never heard the insult before, but Marty went blind mad. He took a running dive at one of the biggest boys in the group. Meanwhile more stones were landing all around me and Chrissie. We tried chucking some back but we were badly outnumbered.

Suddenly I heard a clunking noise just above my left ear followed by a sharp pain drilling through my head. I fell forward onto the path. One of the rocks had hit me full on and knocked me over. As I looked down I could see blood gushing from my arm and leg where I'd sliced them as I fell. More blood was running down the side of my head, soaking my hair all the way down to my shoulders.

I was still lying on the ground when one of the gang came over and punched me clean in the face. He wasn't even a kid, he was a grown man and I was still just a little girl.

'You leave her alone,' Marty shouted, smashing his fists into any of the gang still left hanging around. One by one they finally wandered off.

By the time we turned up back at the site we were all three damp and sticky with blood. Daddy was furious. 'Who did this?' he yelled, over and over again, before launching into Marty for getting into a fight with country people.

Daddy rang the police but they weren't interested. 'Just kids being kids,' they said. But I'd been battered half to death. It took me weeks to recover completely from that beating.

We knew the score though – what happened to travellers didn't matter in the same way as it mattered when it happened to country people. I'd known that since forever. Mammy and Daddy never sat us down and said, 'Look, there's people out there who don't like travellers,' but they didn't need to. We just knew.

When we went into shops Mammy would say, 'Say nothing. Just keep your mouth shut because if they hear your accent they'll know we're travellers and we'll not be welcome.' Mammy was always able to put on her 'posh' accent when she went into shops and garages so no one was quite sure where she came from. Or maybe people did know and we were all just fooling ourselves about Mammy's acting abilities! Lots of country people were fine with us, of course, but still, there were plenty who weren't.

Sometimes in the evenings we'd hear the adults talking about one of them getting 'put out' of a bar or a shop because they were travellers. It's illegal to do that now, although it does still go on. But back in the 1970s, travellers were constantly being booted out of places for no other reason than that the owner didn't want them on his premises.

But like I said, the distrust and dislike wasn't just in one direction. It cut both ways. 'Don't ever trust country people,' Ol'Daddy would tell us time and time again. 'They'll turn on you in a minute.' He meant they'd turn their back on you and be two-faced at any opportunity, calling you names and insulting you, or worse.

The outside world was a place to be treated with the utmost suspicion. Home was safe. But while home for country people is a house and an address, it's not like that for travellers. No, home for us was family.

3

Our Family

If I could have just one word to describe my family it'd be 'noisy'.

Around the time I 'became' Rosie rather than Mud, I went back to living with my parents. I was eight years old and Mammy had got over her fear of me choking and wanted me to come back. We carried on travelling around the north of England, staying in temporary sites on the edges of big towns and cities like Warrington, Wigan, Bradford, then further north to places like Newcastle and Gateshead. Most of the time we travelled with Ol'Mammy and Ol'Daddy, which suited me because then I could spend my every waking hour with Marty and Chrissie. Our trailer was like a household orchestra of Daddy's constant folk music, Bridget's chattering, Kevin's racing car impressions, toddlers gabbling and babies screaming. Oh yes, and of course Mammy yelling at us all to shut up! But I loved those sounds, because they meant home. Mammy and Daddy's trailer was about the same size as Ol'Daddy's with two double bedrooms – one for our parents, one for us girls and a lounge with a fold-down bed for the boys.

I'd loved my time with Ol'Daddy and Ol'Mammy and my parents were almost never more than a few feet away in their trailer but part of me felt I was missing out somehow by being away from them at nighttime. And I loved Daddy so much that by then I wanted to be near him every moment of every day. I felt awful to leave Ol' Mammy and Ol' Daddy, though. For ages I was worried they'd be offended if I moved out of their trailer but when I finally plucked up the courage to say I wanted to go back, they were brilliant. And because our trailers were almost always side by side I still saw them all the time.

By that point, Bridget was 10 and Kevin a gangly 12-year-old. Then younger than me were 'the little'uns': Sean, who was five, Tommy, four, Tina, two and baby Maria. There was three years between me and Sean, the next one down, and that age gap meant that rather than be playmates I was expected to help bring him up and the younger ones too. Bridget's job was to help Mammy with the chores.

Mammy was ultra house-proud, or trailer-proud, I should probably say. Our caravan, which travellers call a trailer, was her castle. Every day without fail she would be tidying, cleaning, dusting and polishing. The walls were painted the 1970s staple shade of magnolia. At the windows were little nets held up with a plastic cord and yellow flowery curtains which Mammy had bought on special offer in British Home Stores then hemmed by hand. At one end of the lounge area was our kitchen, which had a couple of narrow work surfaces for preparing food and a two-ringed hob.

But pride of place, up high on a shelf that ran the entire length of the trailer, was Mammy's Crown Derby collection. At every fair and jumble or boot sale, Mammy would be on the hunt for teacups, saucers, pots and sugar basins in her favourite delicate gold-patterned design. Every morning she would lovingly get down each piece of crockery, dust it gently then replace it. Sometimes a new teapot would be in favour and oust an old milk jug from front row position. Then Daddy might return home with a serving dish that he'd picked up on his travels. For a while that would be the cherished piece, until the next new arrival for her collection.

One afternoon me and Bridget were playing with her Sindy dolls in the trailer. I found brushing their hair and dressing and undressing them mind-numbingly boring so I decided I should try out the doll's gymnastic abilities instead. After a cartwheel and a backflip Sindy went for a triple somersault, flying up in the air and smacking straight into a Crown Derby coffee pot. I could swear that that pot wobbled off the shelf then fell to the ground in slow motion. Before it had even landed in a million different pieces I knew the horror that awaited me.

'Jesus, Mary and Joseph', Mammy screamed, running into the trailer, 'What have you done now Rosie?' There was little time for explanation. I was grabbed by the back of my polo neck sweater and chucked down the trailer steps onto the ground. Mammy didn't often get really mad but when she did you were best well out of her way.

In the corner of our trailer was a black and white portable television. But to be honest, it was more for show than practical use. The reception on the sites was usually so rubbish that after a couple of minutes our eyes would go weird from staring at a screen of snowflakes or vertical lines which kept drifting upwards. Sometimes if there was a 'big event' other families from the site would crowd into our trailer to watch it. They had their own tellys too, but as with everything, travellers prefer to do things together.

One night there was a big boxing match on the telly. I think it was one of Muhammad Ali's last fights and all the men on our site loved Ali. He was a man's man. That evening you could barely get in the front door of our trailer for men yelling at the screen. But the reception was so bad that poor old Paddy Daly, who lived in another of the trailers on the site, spent the entire night outside, twisting the aerial on the back of our caravan one way and then the other to try to pick up a better picture.

'Go on, wallop him, boof, boof,' Ol'Daddy was yelling at the screen.

'Ah shit, Paddy, move that aerial,' my Daddy joined in. 'Ali's just laid the big fella out and now the picture's broke and we'll never know if he's dead or alive.'

Ol'Daddy never did really get to grips with the television and hardly ever watched it. It was just one modern invention too far for him. If we were sat watching a film together he'd be constantly yelling at characters, 'Look out, he's about to bash you,' or 'No, don't get into the car, the brakes have been cut.' Us kids wouldn't be able to stop laughing although we were never quite sure whether he really thought the characters could hear him or whether he just got carried away with the excitement of it all.

Mammy spent all her days looking after Daddy and us kids. I never thought to wonder if that is what she really wanted to do or if she'd ever dreamed of having a job outside the home. That just wasn't what women in our culture did. No, Mammy's job was feeding her family and cleaning. We joked she was a 'cleanaholic'. Turned out in a pair of crisp indigo-blue jeans and tight white t-shirt with her ebony black hair tied back with a clip, she would rampage through the trailer every morning on the hunt for the merest speck of dust. With an Elvis cassette in the tape player, she'd sing along hopelessly out of tune, while scrubbing the floor, bleaching the sink and endlessly dusting her collection of picture frames and, of course, the prized Crown Derby. We might have only had three rooms but it was amazing the time it took Mammy to clean it through every day.

Then, once it was all neat and tidy she'd go into her bedroom and change into her 'afternoon' clothes. Sometimes I'd follow her just to watch the amazing transformation. I was rarely out of jeans with holes in both knees and a stripey sweatshirt that had become so small that it stopped just above my belly button. But even though I hated the thought of wearing skirts and dresses myself, I loved the way Mammy could slip into a frock and instantly become a lady.

When I was nine she had her eighth baby, Jimmy. But within weeks her body had once again snapped back into her incredible size-eight figure. Every afternoon she'd clip up her rosewood (that was what it said on the Clairol packet in the bathroom) coloured hair in heated rollers then leave them to fizz while applying layer after layer of thick black mascara then slashing a bright red line of lipstick across her mouth. When the heated curlers came down and she shook out the curls, she looked like a film star.

Mammy liked things to be 'just so'. And that meant the trailer looking good, her own appearance quite jaw-dropping and her kids polite and respectful. She was strict with us and we knew never to mess about when Mammy was around. She wasn't the kind of mother who'd hug and kiss us much or tell us that she loved us. But she never needed to do any of that. We knew she loved us.

Daddy may have been less strict with us kids than Mammy but, as in most traveller families, the man called the shots. What he said, went. To me, he was desperately handsome, tall and strong with a broad smile that stretched wide across his face. He was always sharply dressed in a suit and tie and leather shoes that Mammy would polish until her hands were stained with the black dye. He worked with Ol'Daddy on the scrap metal lorries but he was always turned out as if he were off for a day's work at the Bank of England. My Daddy was one of the first men around in the early 1980s with a mobile phone, too. He loved 'mod cons' as he called anything more advanced than a tin opener, and Daddy always knew someone who could get him the latest must-have at a good price. His phone was a massive object, so heavy he had to carry it around in a small suitcase but we thought it was incredible, like something out of the "Starship Enterprise!"

Back in those days there was good money to be made in buying and selling scrap that no one else wanted. A lot of country people assume that travellers are poor but I never remember us being short of money. There was always plenty of food in the cupboards, we had smart clothes and at Christmas time it was like Santa's grotto in our trailer.

Daddy was from a different traveller background entirely to Mammy. He'd grown up travelling around Scotland before moving south with his family and meeting Mammy.

His family believed in matchmaking and fortunes. That's not fortune telling, it's the tradition that a bride's family pays a 'fortune' to her husband when they marry. It's like a dowry and the tradition still goes on today in some traveller cultures. Ten years or so ago the typical fortune was around £100,000 to £200,000, but nowadays it's more like £20,000. Each groom is expected to ask for a bit more from his bride than the last man in his family who married, and so the figure is constantly getting pushed higher and higher.

In Daddy's culture of travellers, if a boy went out with a girl three or four times they were said to be 'going steady'. Then after a month or so he'd be expected to ask her to marry him. That's when the girl's family would have to start getting their money ready. If the family couldn't raise the cash there wasn't going to be any wedding, even if the couple were a hundred years of age and madly in love. I don't like the system at all and even as a little girl I hated the idea that women were being bought and sold.

'Mammy, will Daddy have to pay for me to get me married off one day?' I asked once.

'I expect so,' she replied.

'I don't want you and Daddy to sell me, though,' I replied. 'I like it here.'

Mammy never had much time for this kind of questioning. 'Well you, young lady, are going to have to learn to do what's expected,' she said. 'Rather than going round doing whatever you fancy you're going to have to start doing things the traveller way.'

I didn't like the sound of that at all!

Over the years my opinion of this particular traveller custom got worse. I remember much later, when I was a teenager, I made friends with an older girl who was in her mid twenties. She had white blonde hair, pale eyes and looked permanently exhausted. She'd been going out with a fella for ten years and they were desperate to marry but her family couldn't afford the fortune that his family were asking for. They saved and saved and saved, killing themselves working, but they still couldn't scrape enough together. There was no doubt that the boy really loved her but he couldn't persuade his family to let her parents off the huge sum because they desperately needed it to pay for his sister's fortune. It was a vicious circle. But they couldn't run away either because then they'd both be disowned by their families. So my friend got pregnant on purpose which is a terrible scandal among travellers as all women are expected to remain virgins until their wedding night. She thought once she was pregnant the boy's family would have to allow their son to marry her but they still refused. The plan had totally backfired. That meant she faced being a single mother, which among travellers is the ultimate shame. She'd never have been able to marry anyone else. In the end her parents had to sell their caravan and their car and borrow thousands of pounds from relatives in America to finally raise the fortune. Their family was left destitute. All so their daughter could get married and not bring shame on the family. I thought it was madness.

When our Daddy, Tommy McKinley, met Mammy on a site near Bristol back in the mid 1960s, Ol'Daddy made it clear from the start that his daughter was not for sale.

He thought he had the most beautiful daughter in the land and he wouldn't hear tell of the idea that he should have to pay some man to take her off his hands. He thought men should be lining up to pay him for the honour of marrying his precious Theresa.

Ol'Daddy never thought Daddy was good enough for his daughter and initially he refused to agree to the marriage. But Tommy and Theresa had fallen in love by then and decided to run away. When travellers run away it's not the same as when country people do it. In our community, a couple will run away to a relative's trailer and spend the night there, strictly chaperoned in separate rooms. There is no way they would sleep together because that is a total no-no, but the fact that they've even been away from home together overnight brings enough shame on the family that they have to marry immediately.

When Mammy and Daddy came back the morning after their 'running away' Ol'Daddy was apparently furious and ready to beat Daddy's brains out but he still agreed to a wedding just as soon as possible in a nearby church to save Mammy's reputation.

'There'll be no fortune though,' Ol'Daddy snarled.

Mammy and Daddy were a love match and in the early years of my childhood my only memories of them together are good ones. They'd get dressed up and go out dancing or if they were staying in they would cuddle up on the sofa, Mammy crying till she laughed at Daddy's rotten joking around. At family weddings Mammy and Daddy would be the ones starting off the dancing then getting us kids around them in a big circle.

Mammy loved the Loretta Lynn song, 'Coal Miner's Daughter' and they'd dance around the trailer to that, Mammy's head resting on the tip of Daddy's chin. Mammy wasn't as warm and touchy-feely as Daddy but I think she loved the way he enabled her to lose her inhibitions.

It was only much later that I realised that deep down

there may have been a lot more troubles in the marriage
than my child's eyes could see at the time. Back then, I
thought that like me, Daddy thought Mammy was the
most beautiful, stylish woman who'd ever lived. And he
was so handsome, tall and strong that Mammy clearly
adored him in the way she did her father.

We adored Daddy too. While Mammy was always on
our case about tidying up and keeping ourselves clean,
Daddy didn't care two hoots about that sort of thing. If we
wanted to go to the pictures or ride out on our bikes it'd be
Daddy we'd ask. We knew we could always talk him round.
'OK, you can go,' Daddy would say. 'But don't tell your
Mammy I said so!'

Daddy was never a violent man to us but he would fight
to protect his family. Back then there were some groups of
travellers who'd go around from site to site taking people's
lorries and trailers off them. They'd turn up at a place and
intimidate people into handing over their car keys with
threats of beatings and terror.

We'd always been on our guard about people like this
turning up. All the travellers knew of them; they were from
families who'd bash you lifeless as soon as look as you. We
just hoped that we would escape their attention.

Then one day it happened.

Us kids were all hanging around the back of the trailer
when a red van pulled up. It had massive thick wheels and
an exhaust like a jet engine. Three of the roughest fellas I'd
ever seen got out slowly and walked up to Daddy. The fella
in the front had barely a tooth in his head. His ears were
bashed up and his hair was thick with grease.

'I want your lorry,' he said to Daddy.

'Well you're not having it,' came the reply. Me and Bridget stood stone still by the side of the trailer. I could feel myself starting to wheeze and my palms were sweating. This was real bad.

'You know who we are and what we do,' the man replied slowly. 'So just you be handing over your keys.'

'No,' Daddy said quietly again. He wasn't the kind of man to be intimidated by anyone but even though I felt proud of him at that moment I was terrified. About then I felt a hand grab my shoulder and start pulling me backwards into the trailer. It was Mammy yanking me and Bridget inside. 'For the love of God, get in here now,' she hissed. Inside the trailer we joined our brothers and sisters already crushed up against the window watching what was going on.

Daddy and four of the other men from the site were rolling around on the floor with the thugs. I saw one of their boots smash into the side of Daddy's friend, Des Gill's head and a rainbow-shaped plume of blood spurt from his ear. There were arms flailing in all directions and legs kicking, stamping and shuffling. Then I could see an iron bar being flung around and men dodging it as best they could.

It felt like the fighting went on for hours although it was probably only minutes before the three men got back into their truck. The greasy-haired fella wound down his window and spat towards Daddy, 'We'll be back, you know.'

Us kids were cheering in the caravan that our daddies had seen off the men. But they were less happy about their victory. With blood still pouring from their cuts and through rapidly closing-up black eyes, the men hitched our trailers onto the back of the cars and we were gone from that site within hours. The men knew that there was no way they'd be able to see off that gang a second time.

Daddy had learnt to be tough and fend for himself from an early age. His father had died from a heart attack when he was a little boy and his mother had brought up him and his ten brothers and sisters on her own. It can't have been an easy childhood and I think he worked extra hard to give us the attention and material things like toys and sweets which he'd missed out on as a kid.

When her children grew up, Daddy's mother lived with one of his sisters. We didn't see Granny McKinley as much as Mammy's family but we would meet up with her at sites sometimes and stay together for a couple of months or so.

Granny McKinley was a tall, scrawny woman with not an ounce of flesh to spare on her. Her skin was stretched tight over her nose and cheekbones and she could look terrifying to strangers but she was a real comedian with a filthy tongue and a dirty laugh.

I loved sitting with her, with a big mug of tea and a plate of corn bread slathered in jam and listening to her stories. 'Drink up your bread and eat your tea,' she'd giggle. In the evenings Granny McKinley would sew bibs and make pegs that she'd sell at fairs or door to door, but even as she was working she'd be telling stories about her teenage years that would make everyone fall about laughing.

My family was my entire world in a way that I think country people find hard to understand. For years I barely knew anyone who I wasn't related to. The only person who wasn't a blood relative who I spent much time with was Daddy's workman, Sid, God rest his soul.

Most travellers had a workman who helped out on jobs in return for their bed and board. Usually they were country men who were down on their luck like Sid, who lived with us for years and years. He had run away from home as a young boy and lived with my uncle before coming to us. It was a strange life for the workman because although he travelled with us everywhere we went, he always remained slightly apart because he wasn't from our culture.

Workman Sid – which was what us kids called him – was a short, squat man whose face drooped down on one side. He was a bit slow but Daddy always defended him and Workman Sid adored Daddy in return. 'He's a good worker,' Daddy would snap at anyone who looked at him as though he were simple. We were taught to treat him with respect and every night before dinner I'd help Mammy plate up a meal for Sid. I'd then run round to his lorry and give it to him because he never ate with the rest of us, it wasn't the done thing. 'You're a good girl, Rosie,' Sid would say every night as I handed over his dinner, taking good care not to splash the gravy. That was about the most I ever heard Sid say. But there was a kindness in his eyes and I loved him for that. I suppose he'd never known any other way of life. We were the only family he had. During the day Sid would help Daddy work, then in the evenings he'd clean the lorries. At night after his dinner he'd sleep in the back of his lorry, covered in a small mountain of blankets. As a kid I never questioned why our lives were so different. It was only as I grew older that it began to seem strange that we were so separate even though we lived our entire lives on the same plot of land.

4

Home

Moving was our way of life and knowing no other, I loved it. Usually we'd move because Daddy had heard there was good work to be had in a different town. Other times he and Mammy would want to travel to a site to meet up with one of their cousins, or we'd go to visit a sick relative or move on for a funeral. Sometimes we'd be forced to move because the police would put us on our way. A lot of our camps were just at the side of roads or in car parks so after a couple of weeks half a dozen coppers would turn up all heavy handed and we'd know it was time to go. We'd laugh at the coppers in their silly hats and sheets of paper threatening court action unless we moved on within 24 hours and the like. Us kids would be leaning out of the windows watching all the action but it never scared us, it was a way of life. Daddy and the other men on the site would go out to speak to the police then come back up the trailer steps and say, 'Come on, pack everything up, we're leaving in the morning.' There was little point in fighting to be allowed to stay. We knew the law always worked against travellers.

One time our Granny McKinley was staying with us when the police and council officials came to move us on. The policemen were a right pompous pair with their big hats and truncheons, but Granny wasn't worried. Marching straight up to one of them, this scrawny, sour-looking old woman suddenly snatched his hat and baton and started dancing round the site with it. The travellers were falling about laughing, particularly as the copper got more and more irate.

'Bring that back here this minute,' the policeman shouted.

'Only for a kiss,' Granny giggled, puckering up her lips to the young fella.

It must have felt like a lifetime for the poor copper before he finally managed to wrestle his hat back from the old lady taunting him. We loved it because it was a rare occasion when we had the upper hand. Usually we knew we didn't stand a hope in hell of being listened to when the coppers turned up.

Once the police arrived just as Susan Daly, a woman in the trailer across the way from us, was about to go into labour.

'You must be out of here by this time tomorrow,' the police chief shouted around the site, his shiny shoes sinking into a muddy patch in the middle of the trailers.

'But my wife is about to give birth here,' said Mrs Daly's husband, Paddy.

'As I said, you need to be out of here this time tomorrow,' the policeman coolly repeated.

After he left, the men stood around talking while the women got us kids ready for bed.

Next morning we woke up expecting the usual activity that accompanied a move but it was quiet. We were staying – whatever the police said. By teatime the police were back, but this time they had with them huge tractors and two dozen big men from the council. Seeing that we hadn't gone voluntarily, they hooked our trailers up one by one onto their big tractors and dragged them out onto the road. There was nothing we could do. Susan Daly, nine months pregnant and the shape of a hot air balloon, could only stand and watch as her home was yanked off the site. When all the lorries, trucks and trailers had been pulled from the site, the council workers lowered heavy breeze blocks across the entrance. There would be no going back. Then there was a police escort all around us as we set off at a snail's pace to the nearest approved traveller site, eight miles down the road.

By the time we arrived at the new site, Susan was starting to get pains so all the men made themselves scarce as the women gathered inside Susan's trailer to help with the baby. A couple of hours later, Susan emerged on the front step of her van holding a baby boy they named Ronnie. Her hair was a bit matted and her cheeks were flushed but apart from that she looked no more exhausted than if she'd just scrubbed the trailer floor. What a woman!

The council-approved sites were OK I guess but they were busy and we didn't always know everyone there. My daddy preferred to camp by the side of the road surrounded by family and close friends. That is how travellers had always managed in the past and so long as we weren't upsetting anyone else we could never understand why we weren't allowed to carry on living that way. But when I was a kid the laws affecting travellers were changing rapidly and almost all of them made our way of life harder. Moving on to a new site was exciting, though. And we'd almost always find people there that we knew so it wasn't like there were sad goodbyes and new beginnings all the time, it was just a gradual shifting of the same people from place to place.

Then, when I was about ten, Daddy crashed his lorry. He wasn't badly hurt but he was taken to court for careless driving and lost his driving licence for six months. Of course with no driving licence we couldn't travel anywhere but we were also being moved on from the temporary site where we had been stopping near Newcastle. Things were about to change drastically.

'We've got a house,' Daddy announced one day as he stomped into the trailer where me and Bridget were laying the table for tea. All the kids were crowded round waiting for Mammy to slam down their plates of egg and chips on the table but after Daddy's announcement the pushing and shoving stopped and we all stared at each other.

We were totally bewildered. We weren't happy, but we weren't particularly sad either. It was a step into the total unknown.

'It'll only be for a few months, kids,' Daddy said. 'Just till I get my licence back.'

We shut up the trailer and left our cousins to keep an eye on it. Our new house was only just down the road on a council estate in Newcastle so we could pop back any time. But I feared we might never really be back again.

Ol'Daddy did shuttle runs between the site and our new house to get Mammy, Daddy, all eight of us kids and our furniture there. When I turned up at the door I was stunned by the size of the place. It was a big flat-fronted semi-detached council house with four equal-sized windows looking out onto a front lawn split in half by a concrete path which led up to the bottle-green front door. There were red tiles on the roof and a chimney pot. If you'd ever asked a child to draw a picture of a house, this was it. We were going to be living in a proper house.

As more and more of my brothers and sisters piled out of Ol'Daddy's lorry and went inside grappling with mattresses, kettles, blankets and black plastic bin bags full of clothes, we must have looked a right sight. A lot of the neighbours in the street were from traveller families and they were out in their front yards to greet us. I guess the council thought it was a good idea to keep the travellers together, certainly we preferred it that way.

Inside the house, me, Kevin and Bridget went from room to room, touching the walls, jumping on the beds and flicking the on and off switch on the electric fire, watching the fake logs light up then fade away again. The little ones spent hours doing roly-polys off the sofa and across the thick-pile, olive green carpet in the front room. They'd never seen anything so luxurious and soft on a floor in their lives! Perhaps now I wouldn't rate that lurid colour carpet alongside orange and chocolate swirling wallpaper and velour curtains so highly, but at the time it felt like a palace.

But by night time, our sense of excitement with our new home was fading fast. There were four bedrooms, which meant there was plenty of space for all of us to sleep comfortably without being lined up one next to the other. But that became the problem. There was too much space.

'I don't want to go upstairs on my own,' I whimpered.

'Yes, there's probably been loads of people die in here,' joined in Bridget.

'Yeah, died screaming in pain,' added Kevin helpfully.

'We'll all sleep in here tonight,' Daddy said, pointing at the olive carpet.

Mammy hauled in our blankets and we laid down on the floor all together, just like in the trailer. I didn't realise it then but I think Mammy and Daddy were probably just as scared as us kids about being in such a big place with floor-boards that squeaked and walls that creaked in the night. In the trailer we could always hear if someone was walking up to the place after dark, but in a house you'd have no way of knowing if someone was outside. And we weren't surrounded by all our relatives here, either. The way country people lived seemed much more scary to us.

It was while we were living in the house that I realised for the first time how much even some normal non-violent country people disliked travellers. On the sites we were pretty isolated from them, so apart from the occasional encounter like the one me, Marty and Chrissie had in the park with the thugs, we hadn't had much bother. But now country people were our neighbours. One woman a few doors down the street loathed us from the moment we arrived even though she had never even spoken to us.

One afternoon I walked past with Bridget and saw her on her doorstep. 'Why don't you just clear off, you dirty gypos,' she yelled at us. Then she got a bottle of bleach and poured it on the pavement outside her door where we had walked. 'I'll have to clean your filth off this pavement now.'

Me and Bridget just put our heads down and carried on walking. I pretended I hadn't heard a thing and I guessed Bridget was doing the same. Maybe if we both acted as though we hadn't heard it, then it hadn't really happened. But my cheeks burnt with embarrassment and anger.

Finally, after what seemed like an age, Bridget muttered, 'Ol' cow,' and rubbed her eyes with the back of her cuff. Seeing my older sister crying over the insult, I felt tears burn in my eyes too.

When we got home the pair of us were flushed, red-eyed and silent.

'What's up with you two?' Daddy asked.

'Nothin',' I replied, my voice crackling slightly.

'So there is,' Daddy said.

'Isn't,' I snapped. I didn't want to have to repeat what that woman had said, not to my daddy. I knew he'd go clean mad if I did.

'Look, Rosie,' Daddy said, 'if you've done something wrong, just tell me.'

'It wasn't us,' I blurted out. 'It was that ol'woman down the street calling us this and that and then, Daddy, then she said she was going to have to bleach the pavement and me and Bridget, we didn't know where to look and so we kept on walking and why did she say that Daddy, why did she say that?'

Once I'd started talking I couldn't stop. All the hurt and frustration poured out of me.

Daddy put his arm around me and Bridget who by then was sobbing openly. 'Don't you worry yourselves, girls,' he said. 'Now, who do you believe, me or that ol'baggage down the road?'

'You,' we both replied quietly.

'Right,' he said. 'And I'm saying you're the brightest, prettiest, most lovely girls in the whole wide world. And that's the truth.'

But Daddy made sure he got his own back. A few days

later a lorry load of manure was delivered to the old woman's front step! I bet it took a lot of bleach to get rid of the stink of that.

Walking around that estate all the settled kids would shout names at us: 'Gypo' or 'Pikey' but we let it go over our heads. We'd always been told you couldn't trust country people because they would slag us off, and that was exactly what was happening. Living on the estate confirmed all our beliefs.

A couple of months later we were back travelling again. I'm not sure if Mammy and Daddy had initially wanted us to stay in the house permanently but changed their mind when things didn't work out. Whatever their thinking had been, I know we all felt a lot happier when we were back in a trailer.

Daddy part-exchanged our old trailer for a bigger, more modern version. He was always desperate to have whatever was the newest model on the market. We had several different trailers over the years. They were pretty much the same inside, although as the years went by they did get a little bigger and there would be more space for us to sit around the table.

Trailers were hugely expensive and some could be as much as £50,000. But I never heard Mammy or Daddy worried about where money was coming from. Ol'Daddy was quite rich because he'd built his business up from scratch and I think he'd helped my parents get started in life. In those days there was big money in scrap metal, taking something that was worthless to most people then selling it on to workmen who needed it, for a good price. And Daddy was a natural wheeler-dealer. If he had an apple he'd be able to trade it for two oranges and a banana then somehow talk you into giving him the apple back too. So money was never a worry for us.

Daddy liked good things and made sure he had them. His cars were things like Ford Estates and Mercedes and he was constantly exchanging them for something he'd seen on sale that was bigger or newer or had fewer miles on the clock. As well as a car he had a lorry and a pick-up truck. When we moved from place to place, Daddy would drive one of the vehicles, Mammy another and Sid, our workman, the third.

Daddy was always generous with his money. Every Saturday afternoon when me, Marty and Chrissie went off into town to the pictures or ice skating, he'd pull the roll of banknotes out of his pocket, peel off a couple and hand them over to me. 'Here, get yourselves a McDonalds on the way home,' he'd say, 'but remember, don't tell your Mammy.'

Daddy spent a fortune on Mammy's clothes too – although it was never enough for her! 'I haven't got a thing to wear,' she'd moan, obviously overlooking the racks of satin, sequins and shoulderpads stuffed into the double wardrobe in their bedroom.

There were no cheap clothes for Mammy.

Once, Mammy was talking and talking about how she'd been into her favourite little designer shop in town and seen the perfect handbag and shoes to match a silver dress she'd bought for a cousin's wedding.

'Here,' said Daddy, handing her a ward of cash. 'Here's £500, go and get them.'

Mammy snatched the money out of his hand then glared at him in fury. '£500?' she said. I could tell she was getting mad, but couldn't yet understand why. '£500?' she repeated. 'Do you seriously think I can get a decent pair of shoes and a handbag with that?'

Then, honest to God, she took the money and chucked it on our fire.

Us kids burst out in nervous giggles. We couldn't believe what she'd just done and couldn't imagine how Daddy was about to react.

There was the most enormous row between them with shouting and screaming that seemed to go on all night. But come our cousin's wedding, Mammy was there flaunting her new designer silver shoes and handbag. They must have cost poor Daddy a fortune.

It was the 1980s and everyone was being brash with their cash – and Mammy loved that. She may have lived in a two-bedroom trailer, but she had a shoe collection that would have made a millionaire's wife green with envy. There must have been a hundred thousand shoes in our trailer. OK, I'm exaggerating a bit but there was every colour, every style, every heel height, toe shape and designer you could imagine; sandals, stilettos, sling-backs, court shoes, peep-toes and wedges. And then there were the boots; knee-high, thigh-high and ankle. There was a shoe for every occasion. Except of course, according to Mammy, there wasn't the right shoe for any occasion. That's why she was always having to go out and buy a new pair!

In Mammy's culture of travellers there is a huge emphasis on the women looking good. Country people find it hard to get their heads around this. Why would someone spend all that money on clothes but live in a trailer? Why not spend the money on a mortgage, council tax, a

lawnmower and stairs carpet, they think? But being a
traveller is a way of life. A woman who has been born into
that way of life has just as much interest in dressing up
and looking good as any other woman. In fact, very often,
a lot more.

When I was a kid 'the look' for traveller women was sexy
but classy; so there were a lot of pencil skirts and blouses
and of course it was the time of monster shoulder pads so
Mammy was power dressed every time she left the trailer.
Nowadays though, traveller women have taken to wearing
even more revealing and sexy outfits. Some of them think
nothing of turning up at a wedding wearing a micro-mini
and a boob tube. Mammy would never have approved of
that. Traveller women were to look sexy but not cheap.

It drove Mammy to despair that I wasn't interested in
clothes and looking pretty.

'Aw Mammy, can't I just have a pair of jeans?' I'd say
when she came back to the trailer, lugging carrier bags full
of pink and lilac frills and frou-frous. What would I want
with a polka-dot ra-ra skirt? I couldn't ride my Chopper
wearing that. I had quite long legs, dark eyes and thick
black hair and could look quite presentable if I did get
myself dressed up and let Mammy rag up my hair to give it
curls. But most of the time I just couldn't be bothered. I
preferred to keep my hair brushed back off my face and
tied back with an elastic band. And I had no interest in the
beauty potions, lotions and make-up that were beginning
to spread across my older sister Bridget's bedroom shelf.

I was a tomboy through and through.

On sunny days me, Marty and Chrissie would be
outside from dawn till dusk. If it was windy, drizzling or

foggy we'd still be out. And snow only made things more fun. Relentless rain pounding on the trailer roof for hour after hour was the only thing that could keep us shut up indoors. We hated it. And it would drive Mammy utterly demented as we rolled around fighting on her neatly plumped-up cushions. Even telly wasn't much help in keeping us occupied. Even when we could get a picture on the old black and white set, there was rarely anything to watch during the day back then.

On Sunday morning we went to Mass, no matter where we were staying. The first thing Daddy would do when we turned up at a new site would be to nip out and look for the local Catholic church. Religion was a big part of our lives. Because a lot of travellers originate in Ireland and Eastern Europe, Catholicism plays a very important role in the culture. We said our prayers every night and morning. I always found something comforting in those traditions. And of course it was usually the only place we mixed socially with country people. By and large we were accepted in every church we went to. It was a place where we didn't have to feel different. That was nice.

I loved Mass. I enjoyed the routine of the service, maybe because no matter where we were living it was always the same. And I felt close to God there. I never questioned anything about the church or faith. Like the traveller life, it was just the way things were.

The best time of our year was Christmas. It was a huge event in our culture and there couldn't be too much food, booze, tinsel or flashing lights. It was way over the top and that was how we liked it. For Christmas dinner there would be at least four different cuts of meat: a turkey, lamb, beef and a ham. Not to mention the sausages, veggies, roast potatoes and mashed spuds too. Mammy would cook all that in our trailer, goodness only knows how! Sometimes we'd go to Ol'Daddy's for Christmas and there would be 30 or 40 of us there. A huge table would be laid out the length of the trailer and people would come and go as they could find a space to squeeze into. All the women would help out and it was an incredible occasion.

I remember one Christmas me and Kevin were both desperate for bikes while Bridget wanted a Tiny Tears. We were so excited on Christmas Eve that there was no way we could sleep. Then we heard a big box being dumped in the middle of the kitchen area of the trailer.

'He's been,' Bridget whispered. 'Santa, he's been. You've got to go and see what he's brought, Rosie.'

'No way,' I said. 'If he finds out that we've been peeking in the middle of the night he might take it all away again.'

Our belief in Santa was absolute.

'Oh, go on,' Kevin joined in. I knew as the youngest of the three of us, I'd end up having to do it anyway, so I might as well get on with it. I crept out of the bedroom and into the kitchen where I was faced by the world's largest cardboard box. The only way I could peek inside it was by climbing up the side of the bunks. I'd just got to the top of the bunk when I lost my grip and fell head first into the box.

'What on earth is going on in there?' I heard Mammy shout from her bedroom.

'It's only me, Rosie,' I said. 'I'm just getting a slice of bread,' I said, rubbing my head where it had smashed into something that looked suspiciously like a brand-new Chopper bike wrapped in dozens of sheets of Rudolph paper.

The only problem was that now I was in the box, I couldn't get out again. It was lucky Mammy had stayed in bed.

'Bridget, Kevin. Quick, help me,' I hissed.

It seemed an age before my brother and sister finally appeared at the top of the box and pulled me out again. We darted back to bed so relieved Mammy and Daddy hadn't found us. Looking back, I'm sure they knew exactly what we were doing – there was only a thin sheet of plastic between their room and the kitchen. They were probably just killing themselves laughing at my predicament!

There was so much laughter then. Life was simple for us as kids, and simple for us as travellers. It was only as we got older that everything became so much more complicated.

5

Travellers in the Troubles

The Northern Ireland Troubles were still at their height when Daddy thought it would be a good idea for us, a family of travellers, to pitch up on a site just off Belfast's infamous Falls Road. At that time there was only one thing the Loyalists hated more than Catholics – and that was gypsies. But there we were, our car and trailer lurching across the Irish Sea on an overnight ferry crossing in early September 1982. I was twelve years old. The hunger strikes were still going on and Bobby Sands was not long dead. British soldiers and civilians on both sides were getting shot, and skirmishes on the streets of Belfast were a nightly occurrence.

'We'll be fine,' said Daddy, in that way he had of making it feel as though everyone was getting themselves worked up about nothing at all. He had an uncle who was living in Belfast and he'd promised Daddy work if we all came over.

The air was thick with mist as we drove off the ferry but we could see enough to realise that Belfast was a very different place to anywhere we'd travelled before. Soldiers stood on street corners with massive guns that they looked ready to shoot at a moment's notice. Burnt-out cars were abandoned in the streets, and walls of houses had pictures painted on them of men in balaclavas and slogans I couldn't read, let alone understand.

When we arrived at the site it wasn't yet nine o'clock in

the morning and the mist was still hanging over the trailers. But we didn't have so much as a pint of milk to make tea so Mammy, Daddy and Kevin went off into town for some shopping, leaving me and Bridget in charge of the little'uns.

'And when we get back I want all these bags unpacked and this place spotless,' were Mammy's parting words as she clip-clopped down the trailer steps looking like a movie star in a bright pink dress she'd chosen specially for the journey and a new pair of black stilettos with a tiny bow at the heel.

Me and Bridget were used to Mammy's high standards when it came to cleanliness. Our life was shaped by instructions such as, 'Don't touch them windows with your mucky fingers', or 'Take those shoes off before you come in here'. But after a night of being tossed around on the ferry, neither of us was in the mood for housework. We knew there was little choice though so we let the little'uns outside to play on the grass while we started unpacking the pots and breakables that were stowed away for safety each time we moved on. Within five minutes someone was banging on the trailer door. I opened it and looked out to see a scrawny looking girl with wiry red hair and a face so covered in freckles that she looked like she'd been burnt.

'Yous coming out to fight?' the girl said.

I looked at her, at first not quite sure that I'd heard her properly.

'Er, no, you're alright,' I replied, feeling my throat tense up and my chest starting to wheeze.

'Yes, y'are,' she said. 'Y'are coming out here right now and we're going to fight.'

I'd never had anything like this before at other sites we'd

stayed at. And after all the tales of leprechauns and friendly giants that Ol'Daddy had filled our minds with over the years, this really wasn't what I'd been expecting of Ireland at all.

'Who're you?' I said.

Ignoring me, she carried on. 'We're going to fight, we're going to fight NOW.'

'Whadda you want to fight for?' I said. I was a tomboy alright and I'd fought enough with my brothers and sisters over the years to know how to look after myself in a scrap, but I didn't want to be doing it now with a total stranger. And anyways, Mammy would kill me when she found out! 'Look, why dontcha just get lost,' I said, slamming the door in her face.

I was half expecting more knocking but everything went quiet and me and Bridget finished tidying up the trailer. Afterwards we decided to take the little'uns for a walk around the site to see who else was staying there. We thought our Uncle John-Joe was there and some of Mammy's cousins too. I changed into my new white drain-pipe jeans and a white top with a sequinned butterfly on the front that Mammy had bought me from Tammy Girl. She said it was always important to look good when you arrived at a new site. 'We've got to show 'em that we've got class,' Mammy would say.

But Bridget and I had barely got round the end of the trailer when the wiry-haired girl reappeared in front of me. This time she didn't say a word. She just walked up and punched me full in the face.

I fell straight to the ground, my white jeans sinking into a pothole of mucky brown water. They were ruined and

Mammy was going to be mad. That put me in a temper. I lashed out and belted the girl square in the jaw and followed it up by yanking her frizzy hair as hard as I could. She fell onto the ground too and I rolled on top of her, holding her down with one hand while I walloped her with the other.

After a couple of minutes I could see she had given in so I got up and ran back to the trailer with Bridget. I had to get those white jeans soaking in Vanish before Mammy got home!

Daddy was still out with Kevin. He'd dropped Mammy off with the shopping saying he'd be back in an hour. As soon as she opened the door to our trailer all my bravery just disappeared and I burst into tears. 'Mammy, she beat me. And I hadn't done nothing. I hadn't.' Mammy could see the red slap mark on my face and the cut on my lip. She knew I'd only fight someone if I'd been seriously provoked, and she was furious.

A couple of minutes later there was another knock at the door. It was the red haired girl's mammy, her two aunts, two sisters and another woman. My mammy went over to the door and flung it open. She was already fired up.

'Get that wee bitch of yours out here,' the women were screaming. 'She can fight our Cilla's big sister if she thinks she's so tough.'

They were what Mammy would call 'rough women', the type who thought kids fighting was a good idea and even encouraged it.

'I will not send my child out there,' Mammy snapped. 'She's a weak chest and could choke herself at any moment. Now leave her be.'

But that was no good for these women. If Mammy

wasn't prepared to let me fight, then she would have to do it instead. And so, in her new black stilhettos with the little bow and the cerise dress that she'd had hanging in the wardrobe for the past month, ready for this journey, Mammy went into battle.

Me and Bridget's mouths made wide 'O' shapes on the trailer window as we pressed our faces up to it in amazement and horror. We'd never in our lives known Mammy to fight before. But there she was now, rolling around in the muck outside with this fat old woman with hair even redder and frizzier than her daughter. She was probably a good three stone heavier than Mammy and she nearly crushed her.

We watched, terrified, as the little split at the back of Mammy's dress stretched into a tear and then into a gaping great hole until it ran all the way up to her white lace knickers. But Mammy never gave up, she slapped and pinched and scratched with all her energy. And then we heard a horrible scream: the fat woman had bitten off some of Mammy's earlobe! And she'd taken with it one of her favourite pearl drop earrings that Daddy bought her a year last Christmas. Blood poured from the side of Mammy's head until the right shoulder of her dress had turned from cerise pink to a lurid red.

Clutching her ear and blinking back tears, Mammy teetered back up the trailer steps. Her dark hair, normally kept under close control by lashings of Elnett, was sticking out in all directions, her dress was destroyed and half her ear was missing. But incredibly she'd kept her stilettos on throughout the whole thing. And they were hardly scuffed.

Me and Bridget washed Mammy's ear and bandaged the wound. She was shaking with anger and still too shocked to cry. Daddy got back to the trailer and found us all in a terrible state. He'd barely had time to ask what in God's name was going on before we heard the third knock at the door. And this time it was the men. With iron bars. And sticks. And bricks.

Daddy was a brave man and he would never run from anything. He knew he stood no chance against these thugs but he went out and took his beating anyway. Mammy kept us away from the window but when he came back in the trailer door he was cut and battered. I think it was only that he'd gone out so bravely and faced them without whimpering that saved him from being beaten to a pulp.

Daddy hitched up the trailer and we were out of that site less than a couple of hours after we'd arrived. Maybe Ireland wasn't going to be such a good place for us to be after all. We only found out later that the daddy of the girl who I'd fought 'ruled' the Belfast travellers. Apparently no one did anything without his say-so, but I'd found that out way too late.

For a couple of weeks we stopped in lay-bys and side roads all around the north of Ireland before finally we pitched up alongside some cousins in a car park back near the Falls Road. The car park was covered in caravans with hundreds of travellers from all over Europe and dozens of different traveller cultures.

Belfast was the first place that I ever went to school. As a little'un I'd gone to a nursery for a few weeks in Leeds or Liverpool or somewhere like that. I remember playing pass the parcel and having a great time, but by the time it came to learning our ABC, we were long gone onto the next site. In Belfast a special school for traveller kids had been set

up. There were a lot of travellers in the city at that time and
the powers-that-be obviously thought it was better for us
all to be educated together. They said it was so they could
cater for our 'diverse learning needs' but I reckon they
probably just didn't want us mixing with the kids from the
posh part of town. In the morning a bus would stop for us
at the end of the road and the half a dozen kids from our
site would climb on, to be greeted by the terrifying faces of
traveller youngsters from all over the city. And some of
those kids were very tough. That bus was like a riot zone.
By the time we pulled up at school there would have been
at least three or four fights. Boys would walk down the
steps with bloody noses and girls would be still clutching
clumps of hair they'd ripped out of an opponent's head.
The bus driver had long ago given up trying to keep any
order on that trip and now his sole intention was to get us
there at breakneck speed so there was the least possible
time for his bus to get totally trashed.

I dreaded that journey and used to shake as I climbed up
the steps onto the bus. I tried to keep a low profile and
would sit squashed right up to the window with my little
brothers Sean and Tommy on either side of me and my
little sister Tina on my lap like a shield. That way it was a
bit more of a struggle for anyone to get close enough to
punch me in the head.

When we arrived at school we were separated into class-
rooms depending on our age. But there seemed to be no
hurry to actually teach us anything. We'd spend a couple
of hours colouring in pictures before trooping into a
canteen area for a cup of watery tomato soup and a slice of
bread. Then after that we were supposed to go to sleep on

the floor for a while. Anyone who did go to sleep got a sweet but even that wasn't incentive enough for most of the people there.

My big achievement at the Belfast Travellers School was learning to spell the word, 'station'. I think it must have been a fluke, or maybe I just repeated what the teacher had said because even though by then I was 12 years old, I still couldn't read or spell far simpler words than that. No matter, I was presented with a lollipop for my efforts. Not that I wanted it; I knew that'd only mean another punch to the head on the bus home. I was right. 'Teacher's pet,' spat a real rough kid called Stevie Quinn, smashing his fist into my ear without even stopping as he walked up the bus gangway that evening.

The journey home followed a depressing routine. If I'd answered any questions in class or tried to make the merest effort as our teacher sounded out the letters of words, I'd be punished on the bus by Stevie or any one of the other kids. 'You think you're right clever dontcha?' they'd say. 'Reckon you're some kind of country girl do you?'

I'd feel the tears burning in my eyes but I knew I couldn't let them show. If I made myself a victim Stevie and his mates would just be back for more, time and time again. I dug my bitten fingernails as deep as I could into the palms of my hands to keep my mind off crying. And I didn't tell. Not Mammy, nor the teachers. I'd learnt by then that like a lot of things, it was just the way things were. It was my problem and I had to deal with it. At night though, I'd lay in bed and touch the bruises on the side of my head and relive every moment of my beating until tears rolled down the side of my neck and into my pyjamas. Then I'd think through what I should have said, what I should have done and imagine what I'd definitely do next time. I never did it of course, but it helped to dream.

Things only got worse when Mammy took me to the opticians who said I needed to wear glasses. Hardly any traveller kids wore glasses and my enemies on the school bus obviously thought it was me trying for a more intellectual look! 'Oi four eyes, whatcha got windows in front of your face for?' came the insults every day.

I hated wearing the glasses and when no one was looking I'd snap the arms off then carry them home to Mammy. 'Stevie Quinn knocked my glasses off,' I'd say. 'And now I won't be able to wear them any more.'

But Mammy was adamant I should be able to see properly and promptly trotted off to get me another pair.

I was on my third pair when Mammy said, 'Break these and you'll get a hiding you won't forget.' I decided the name-calling and hair-pulling and general abuse from the other kids was preferable to being on the wrong end of Mammy's temper, so that pair of glasses stayed safe.

I worked out that the best way to avoid a beating on the way home was to make no effort with my reading and writing, to answer no questions and to show not a flicker of interest in anything. What was the point of learning stuff anyway? I didn't need to be able to read to be a good traveller wife and that was the only future I could imagine. And Mammy and Daddy couldn't read or write and there was nothing wrong with them, I'd tell myself. So I buried any spark of enthusiasm for learning that I'd had and whiled away the hours at school colouring in and chatting with my only friend, Mary Finney, who had an

Adam Ant ruler and the most amazing collection of gorgeous smelling rubbers.

Every Monday morning we would be ordered to line up outside the headmaster's office then have to go in one by one.

'Ah, Rosie McKinley,' he'd say. 'Did you go to Mass yesterday?'

'Yes Sir, I did.'

'And what was the Priest's message?'

That was the tricky bit. Because even though we almost always went and I actually enjoyed Mass, remembering what the priest had talked about 24 hours later would be a struggle for anyone.

'Er, the martyrdom of the saints?' I ventured.

'No Rosie, yesterday was Trinity Sunday so the homily was about the mystery of God the Father, God the Son and God the Holy Spirit. Now put your hand out.'

I knew what was coming next. With a loud thwack the headmaster's cane came slapping down onto my palm. Tears immediately sprang up in my eyes and I rubbed them away with the sleeve of my jumper. I hated crying in public and I made sure there was no sign of tears when I walked back out of his office, the throbbing pain from my left hand shooting up my arm. 'Ol' bastard,' I muttered, just loud enough for other kids in the queue to hear.

Going to school could be a pretty dangerous activity, but it was nothing compared with being at home at night in our trailer. We knew travellers were hated most places they went but it was made so much worse in Belfast because almost all of us were Catholic.

'If anyone asks you what religion you are and you know

for certain they are a Catholic, you must tell them you're Catholic,' Mammy told us. 'But if someone you don't know asks, you say you don't know what you are.'

It was all a bit confusing but we'd heard the stories of travellers getting beaten up by Loyalist gangs and we knew to beware of country people in Belfast more than anywhere else we'd ever been.

Sometimes me and Bridget would walk down The Falls and chat to the soldiers with their big guns. They were always dead friendly to us. One of them was from Leeds and knew the site where we'd lived – even the stretch of pavement where I was born! I think he liked talking to us because we reminded him of home. The Catholics in Belfast were normally friendly to us, too. Sometimes a country man would drive up to the site and ask Daddy to help clear a house that had been bombed out. There would be old bits of furniture that could be flogged on or scraps of metal that would make a few quid. But there were plenty of people who hated us.

One night we were sat in the trailer watching the flickering black and white telly when an orange flash filled the room.

'Get down,' yelled Daddy, and we flung ourselves on to the floor. We could hear shouting outside and I clung onto Bridget, our faces pressed into the floor tiles. A couple of seconds later there was another flash and the noise of glass shattering. Women were screaming and men were shouting and cursing.

Despite Daddy's warnings to stay on the floor, we were right behind him when he opened the trailer door. Outside, about 30 feet away, one of the trailers was blazing. When fire takes hold in a caravan it can be just minutes before the whole lot goes up. Loyalists had been chucking petrol bombs into the camp and one had gone clean through the window of the caravan and started the fire.

The couple that lived in the trailer had managed to carry their three kids out only seconds before the blaze really took hold and their home melted in front of their eyes.

Men from the site went racing after the Orangemen who'd been throwing the petrol-filled bottles. If they'd found them they'd have been torn limb from limb but they were already long gone.

The next morning all that was left of the burning caravan were its metal supports. Everything else had totally burned away. The family moved in with some cousins of theirs who were on the same site but they left Belfast soon after.

In the summertime we travelled down to the south of Ireland and parked up near a beach. Those holidays were some of the happiest times I can remember. Me, Kevin and Bridget would go off on our own for hours on end, investigating rock pools and tiny caverns along the beach, or we'd go fishing with Daddy. Then we'd come back and build sandcastles with the little'uns.

Sean and Tommy were coming up for ten and nine at the time and they were both obsessed with Manchester United. I'd get roped into recreating Man U matches on that strip of sand with them but of course while they were Bryan Robson and Ray Wilkins, I was stuck in goal. The younger girls, Tina and Maria, were less excited about football. Tina was so stick thin she could have passed for one of the goal posts but she was more than happy to stand around and watch the big brothers she adored. Maria tried to be interested but after ten minutes she'd be off wandering

down to the sea in her normal daydreamy state. As for
Jimmy and Paul, who were coming up four and two, they
were happy enough making mud pies and paddling their
chubby toes in the freezing cold sea.

At the end of the day we'd go back to the site where we
were staying and Mammy would barbecue fish with a big
pot of mash. It was the best of times. After six weeks though
it was back to reality and we travelled north again to Belfast.

Back in Belfast the rocks and petrol bombs came flying
into our site most nights, chucked by teenagers who then
ran off into the darkness. No one was ever killed or seriously injured but it was terrifying.

Many times the police or army would drive up to the site
in the middle of the night and go round the trailers banging
on doors. 'Get your families in your cars now and get out
of here,' they would say. 'There's trouble planned.' Me and
Bridget would wrap the little'uns up in blankets and lift
them into the back of Daddy's car and we'd drive 15 miles
out of town to a layby where we'd try to sleep all lying on
top of each other until it was thought to be safe to return
to the site.

We'd also get Orangemen parading past the site in their
sashes and bowler hats during the marching season. I
never could understand it. There they were, all preened
and pumped up, then they'd be hurling rocks at us and
shouting, 'Get out of here you fucking gypos.'

'Just ignore them,' Daddy grunted. It was nothing we
hadn't heard before.

In the end though, Mammy had enough of the bombs
and shootings and insults. 'Come on Tommy,' she said one
morning. 'Let's go back to England.'

Mammy missed Ol'Daddy and her family and she wanted to go home. Home, for her, was always wherever Ol'Daddy was. Daddy had gone over to Belfast for work but he knew he could pick up jobs wherever he went and he was about ready to go back to England too.

By then Ol'Daddy and Ol'Mammy were living in a council house near Manchester. Ol'Daddy felt he was getting older and wanted somewhere warm and dry during the long winter months. I'm not sure how he did it but he managed to pull enough strings to get us the house right next door to them. So we weren't just going back to England, we were going back to a house too.

At first we weren't sure about going back to a house again. We loved being out on the open road but I think Mammy also quite liked the idea of somewhere that her Crown Derby wouldn't get jiggled around every time we went over a pothole! And there would be a garden too. For years Mammy had dreamed of being able to plant out little pots by her front door. But best of all for Mammy and the rest of us was that we'd be close to Ol'Daddy again.

'Families should be together,' Mammy always said. That was what we all believed.

6

Ol' Daddy Dies

By the time we moved back to England I was looking after my younger brothers and sisters most of the time even though I'd only just turned 13. By then there were nine of us altogether and with six of them being younger than me it was pretty much a full-time job.

My elder brother Kevin worked with Daddy out collecting scrap and Bridget helped Mammy with the cooking, cleaning and washing. For years Mammy had done washing by hand outside our trailer in the tin bath or if it was sheets, she'd take them to a local launderette. But after we moved into the house, Daddy came home from work one night and with a great flourish, shoved a twin-tub washing machine into the kitchen. Mammy looked at it with a brisk nod of approval. Mind you, if Daddy had turned up at home with the Crown jewels she wouldn't have looked that much more impressed. But when he came home the next night to find Mammy hauling sheets in and out of her new machine surrounded by steam and scalding water, he could tell she had fallen in love with it!

Our new house was pretty similar to the one we'd lived in briefly in Newcastle. It was a council semi with large rooms and four bedrooms upstairs, which meant we all had plenty of space. Mammy's only dilemma was how on earth she was going to find the time to clean such a mansion!

In the evenings we'd always be visited by uncles, aunties and cousins who were living nearby and the grown-ups would sit around drinking tea and telling stories. Travellers didn't believe in drinking alcohol at home in those days so it was pot after pot of tea.

On a Sunday after dinner Mammy and Daddy might walk down to the local pub, The Drum, for a couple of drinks, leaving me and Bridget to look after the little'uns. But the most Mammy would have would be two vodka and Cokes. 'That's enough for me,' she'd giggle. 'Otherwise I'll be dancing my way home.'

Daddy didn't drink much either. Some of the traveller men were big boozers and would come home stinking of beer and with a foul temper on them, but Daddy wasn't like that. If he did have a few too many he was a jolly drunk whose stories just came faster and faster, more exaggerated with every telling.

Although we were living in a house, we still went off travelling every now and again when the mood took Daddy. We might go off to one of the gypsy fairs like Appleby in Cumbria, where 30,000 gypsies and travellers get together for a long weekend in June, or other fairs in Wales or Scotland and sometimes we might travel a couple of days to see a circus, but most of the time we were settled. That didn't mean we'd become country people though. Oh no, we were still travellers and proud of it. That was our culture and all our friends were travellers too. We still spoke some gypsy words between ourselves, we respected our elders and women wouldn't have dreamed of swearing or work-ing or challenging their men in any way.

When we moved into our house, Workman Sid was given

a council flat near us. He still worked with Daddy during the day but in the evenings he'd sit in his flat on his own, watching the telly. It was strange really because he wasn't a traveller but he found settling down harder to cope with than all of the rest of us. I think he was lonely.

He had his own two-ring hob and a microwave oven in his flat and Daddy would go round there with carrier bags full of dinners that he could just heat up in a couple of minutes. But Sid seemed to be getting thinner and thinner all the time.

One night as Mammy prepared to serve up dinner I put an extra plate in the oven to heat up.

'What're you doing?' Mammy asked.

'I'm just going to plate up a dinner for Sid,' I said. 'You know, like we used to do.'

Carefully I heaped up a pile of stew, mashed potatoes and the great chunks of carrot he'd always loved. Then I wrapped the whole lot in tin foil, slipped my coat on and walked the ten minutes round to Sid's, holding the plate. And I still didn't spill the gravy!

'Ah, you're a good girl, Rosie,' Sid said, just like old times, when I held out the plate to him on the doorstep.

After that I'd run round with Sid's dinner whenever I could. I hated the thought of him there in that flat all on his own, surrounded by his own people at last but more alone than he'd ever been. 'I can't get used to this place,' he would say to Daddy.

We'd only been settled in Manchester six months when Daddy went to call for Sid one morning and found he'd collapsed and died from a heart attack.

Workman Sid had never talked about family and we had

absolutely no idea where he even came from. Daddy spent hours with the police trying to track down any living relatives. Of course Daddy couldn't read or write so the police had to help him go through all Sid's letters and papers to find any clue of where his family might be living. Finally they traced Sid's sister, who was living in America.

She flew over for the funeral and Bridget and I were beside ourselves with excitement. We'd never seen a real live American before although we knew just how they looked, talked and sang from the amount of trash telly we watched on our new *colour* TV. (Oh yes, we were definitely going up in the world!) But Sid's sister was a crushing disappointment. She looked every bit as tanned and glossy as we'd hoped. Just like Pamela Ewing in Dallas. But she was very posh and was pretty snooty towards us. It was pretty clear she was embarrassed that her brother had ended up working for a family of travellers. We'd been far more of a family to Workman Sid than she had ever been, but she still turned her nose up at us and didn't even join us for a drink after the cremation.

Traveller funerals are always big events with thousands of people travelling hundreds of miles to pay their respects at the graveside. But this posh woman from Chicago wanted her brother cremated in a quiet little service as if she were ashamed of him. We couldn't understand it. I missed Workman Sid. He'd been part of my childhood, and now he was gone.

A couple of months after Sid died, me and Bridget were playing out on our bikes and popped in to see Ol'Daddy next door. Usually he was delighted to see us and had the packet of Penguins open before we'd even got through the door. But this time he barely moved off the chair when we walked in and even though he said as usual, 'How ya doin' there girls?' he carried on staring at the fire in the grate.

'We're alright Ol'Daddy,' I replied. 'But how about you?

That seemed to jolt him back into life. 'I'm grand,' he said. 'Now, come and sit up here y'all,' he said. Me and Bridget were by then way too big for sitting on laps but with Ol'Daddy we still did it and he could still just about manage to squeeze us both on his knee. I know Ol'Daddy loved us all but I felt so special when I was with him. As if really, everything he said, was just for me. But that day he looked a bit strange and sad. Then he said, 'Now girls, I've got something to tell you, I'm afraid I won't be here much longer. I'm going to be leaving you.'

Me and Bridget both thought he must mean he'd got sick of the house and was going to be travelling on somewhere without us.

'When are you going Ol'Daddy?' I asked.

'Soon,' he said. 'I won't see our Patsy's baby born.' Auntie Patsy was due to have the baby any day so he obviously meant pretty quickly.

'But why are you moving on without us?' Bridget demanded.

'My time's up,' he said quietly. 'I'm going to die.'

'God forgive you, Ol'Daddy,' I shouted. 'You are not going to die. It'd break Mammy's heart. And what about us?'

Then he shook his head and smiled at us again. 'Ah, ignore me,' he said. 'Now, did I ever tell you about the Irish giant who was so angry he flung a rock all the way over to England?'

He was back to telling his stories again and joking with

us. But I wasn't a kid who believed in fairy stories any more. I was 13 and could tell when things weren't right. I'd been brought up as his own daughter really, for the first eight years of my life. I knew him so well and the pair of us were so close. This time I had a horrible feeling that things were very wrong.

Less than a week later, Ol'Daddy lay dead in a crumpled heap at the side of the road. It had been such a good night in the pub. Ol'Daddy had gone for a couple of pints up The Drum with some of his traveller mates. They met up once a week for a chat and a laugh. Ol'Daddy loved it, although he never got roaring drunk, not like some of the fellas.

'I'm fitter and faster than all you young fellas put together,' Ol'Daddy laughed as they rolled out of The Drum that night.

'Sure y'are, old man,' some of the youngsters laughed back.

'Come on then, I'll beat the lot of you,' he retaliated. And as they jumped into their cars desperately searching for keys to start their ignitions, Daddy was sprinting off into the darkness, just as he'd always done. That was quite an ordinary end to an evening at The Drum for Ol'Daddy and his pals. Usually, ten minutes later they'd all be in the road outside our house, play-fighting, bantering and killing themselves laughing, totally oblivious to the tutting and eye-rolling of their wives and all our neighbours.

Except this time, there was no laughing at the end of the night. And for a while it felt like there would be no laughing ever again.

I was fast asleep in bed, lying next to Bridget, when the sound of screaming woke me. It was Ol'Mammy in the street outside. Usually she rarely spoke so I knew this was bad. Real bad.

Ol'Daddy had been crossing the road in the darkness on his run back home to the site when he had been hit by a bus. His huge body was smashed up and he was clinging to life.

Me and Bridget climbed over our younger sisters in the bed and joined the growing crowd outside. All around there were men and women crying.

Ol'Mammy was sitting on the ground, wailing and screaming. Next to her was our Mammy, clinging on to her. Mammy's face looked utterly blank.

'Come on, we've got to get to the hospital,' Daddy was saying. 'They might still be able to do something. He's as strong as a bull, he'll pull through.'

I was a teenager by then and quite old enough to understand about death and dying but I still couldn't believe this was happening. Not now, not to Ol'Daddy.

As usual I was left to look after the little'uns while Kevin, Bridget, Mammy, Daddy, Ol'Mammy and half the street sped off to the hospital in a convoy of cars, trucks and lorries. When they got there they were told Ol'Daddy was in a coma and haemorrhaging badly. His mass of visitors and well-wishers lined the corridors and waiting rooms, desperate for any news of the man who'd been so loved and respected.

At home I laid on the bed all night listening to the babies sleeping and praying for Ol'Daddy to pull through. Every time I thought I heard a car driving on to the site, my stomach would tense and I leapt up to the window. But by dawn no one had returned home.

The next morning I woke my brothers and sisters and broke the news to them. They loved their granddaddy as much as me and we said our prayers that he'd be saved as we waited for a phonecall from the hospital.

Mammy didn't come home all the next day or the day after. Daddy and Kevin popped back a couple of times to check we were OK but the news of Ol'Daddy was bad.

'Your Mammy thinks you should stay here,' Daddy told me. 'Ol'Daddy's face is smashed up real bad and she doesn't want you to see him like this.'

On the third day I was pegging out some washing in the back yard when I heard a convoy of cars and trucks coming up the road. In the first car was Mammy, Ol'Mammy and Daddy. I knew then. If they were coming home without Ol'Daddy then he must have died.

When Mammy got out of the truck she looked broken. Her hair was hanging loose around her face and there were stains down the front of her silver top. I went to hug her but she only put her hand limply on my back before walking in the front door of our house and immediately shutting herself in her bedroom.

No one had been stronger than Ol'Daddy but even he hadn't been able to battle back from the injuries he'd suffered. The driver whose bus had hit him had been arrested for drink driving. Our hearts were broken.

I don't know whether Ol'Daddy had a foreshaw, which is what travellers call a premonition, of his death or whether he was just feeling old that day he talked to me and Bridget. He was only 53 years old when he died. We'd thought he would live forever.

The next day, Mammy didn't leave her bed. She refused

to eat a thing. 'I just can't face it, Tommy,' she'd say whenever Daddy went in trying to tempt her with a sandwich.

All day long hundreds and hundreds of travellers from all over the north of England turned up next door at Ol'Mammy's house to pay their respects to Ol'Daddy who was laid out in the front room. They queued down the hall to go in, kiss him on the forehead and say a proper goodbye which was the traveller way. By the time I went in to say my goodbye a lady had been in to 'do him up real good' as Mammy said. Powder had been put on his face to cover the bruises but he still looked nothing like the man who had carried me round our site like a carthorse. For me, the pale cold stranger on the drop-leaf table in Ol'Mammy's front room was just a poor imitation of my great Ol'Daddy.

It was left to Daddy to sort the funeral. Ol'Daddy's position in the traveller community meant his send-off had to be grand, it had to do justice to the man he was. Ol'Daddy had wanted to be buried in Ireland so the next day Mammy, Ol'Mammy and Daddy set off to take his body back 'home'. He hadn't lived there for more than 30 years but in the traveller tradition that didn't matter – home was where he belonged. Dozens of other travellers followed behind the car carrying Ol'Daddy's coffin in their cars and trailers. The ferries over to Ireland were packed with travellers going over for the funeral. Mourners came from Germany, Italy and even America.

Me, I was left at home again, minding the little'uns.

I wanted to say goodbye to Ol'Daddy too but I knew better than to argue, particularly given how upset Mammy had been. So for four days I was left alone looking after

Sean, then ten, Tommy, nine, Tina, eight, Maria, seven and the youngsters, Jimmy, four and Pauly who wasn't yet two.

They were great kids but it wasn't easy. The boys were close in age and the moment my back was turned they'd either be punching each other's lights out or hatching some terrible badness. Tina was a skinny little thing then, with kneecaps that jutted out like hammer heads. She was never more than two steps behind me though, helping keep the place tidy, putting a wash on, getting Jimmy and Paul dressed in the mornings and running up the shop every time we ran out of another bag of oven chips. Maria had long red hair with a round face and looked like she should be in an advert for soap or washing powder or something. She was always pretending to be a princess or a fairy or something equally unlikely, which was grand to watch but didn't really help get tea on the table.

Jimmy had a crew cut and was as skinny as Tina. There were two years between him and Pauly but his baby brother followed him everywhere and copied his every move. When the pair of them sat on the sofa to watch cartoons they looked like a couple of old fellas watching the racing down the betting shop.

Nowadays the neighbours would have social services round if they thought a teenager was being left to look after that lot, but in our culture it was the norm. And with everything that was going on, I wouldn't have thought to complain. At times like that, family pulled together and I knew that was what I had to do too. My cousin's wife was supposed to look in on me every now and again to check everything was alright but for the first three days I never saw sight nor sound of her. But although it might have been a bit chaotic, I managed it. I think a lot of people don't have any idea what a 13-year-old is capable of.

I cleaned, changed nappies and made the baby's bottles. I cooked proper dinners.

At night I had all the kids lined up in the bed with me on one side. But the first night I got into bed I put Pauly on the edge, thinking, 'he won't roll far, he's too big for that.' We'd only been in there a few minutes when I heard a thud, followed by screaming. The others had all rolled over and pushed the baby out!

By the fourth day I was exhausted. The house was becoming a tip where the kids were running wild, pulling things off worktops and out of drawers and I'd run out of the energy to keep clearing up after them. At one point the baby's nappy was dirty but he was screaming for a bottle so I was trying to make that up first. It was all going off and then the doorbell rang. Finally my cousin's wife had turned up. She took one look around the house and said, 'You need to get this place cleaned up before your Mammy gets home.' Then she spun round and stomped off, leaving me with it all again. I was spitting mad.

Meanwhile, over in Ireland, thousands of travellers had gathered for Ol'Daddy's funeral. They had lined the streets outside the church where a funeral Mass was said then gathered outside every pub in his small hometown for a drink to remember him. Every bar was packed to overflowing with people lifting a drink for my grandfather. Even people who didn't know him had turned up, that was the tradition, to show respect for a man who had a good name in the traveller community.

When my family finally returned home after five days

away, Mammy looked even more ill than when she'd left. She came straight in the door and went back to bed. I knew how bad she must be when she didn't even glance at the dirty pots in the sink and piles of rubbish all around the place.

Mammy's baby wasn't due for another two months but within weeks she had started suffering pains. They grew worse and worse until she was rushed to hospital and told the baby was already well on its way – but a worrying eight weeks early. This was to be her tenth baby and I think she was feeling too old, tired and sad to be doing it all over again. When Ol'Daddy died it was like a part of her went to. And even when she knew the baby was coming early and might be at risk, she just went through with it all, showing no emotion at all.

Baby Danny was born weighing just over 2lbs. He had a hole in his heart, problems with his lungs and his bowels. A priest was called to the labour ward immediately to baptise the child as doctors feared he wouldn't survive. Mammy cried when she held the baby for the first time but no one knew if she was crying for the baby or because she knew her Daddy would never see the child.

I of course was at home looking after the little'uns as usual but Daddy went backwards and forwards to the hospital where Mammy sat by the baby's cot, day after day, as he slowly but steadily gained strength.

Danny's condition was serious, though. Doctors diagnosed a genetic condition that meant he'd never be able to walk or talk properly. He would need constant care. When Mammy finally came home from hospital with him after three weeks, she simply handed him to me and went back to bed. Her baby had survived but I think she was just too broken to cope with the situation. From that moment on I knew Danny was my responsibility.

Nowadays Mammy might have been diagnosed as having postnatal depression, particularly with such a traumatic birth coming so quickly after the death of her father. But at the time she was left to fend for herself. The problem was, for the first time ever Mammy couldn't cope with what life was hurling at her. And Daddy and us kids had no idea how to make things better.

Before, Mammy would be up at the crack of dawn making Daddy's fry-up, and mopping down the kitchen floor. Now Daddy made his own tea in the morning and the lino tiles were patterned with muddy footprints. She stopped dusting her Crown Derby and pots sat in the sink waiting to be washed from breakfast time until supper. Our Mammy, who'd always raced around the trailer like a cleaning devil, now preferred to sit on the couch staring out the window or just lying in bed.

When she did get up she sat in a pair of baggy grey towelling trousers and a sweatshirt. Her Alexis Colby wardrobe was unopened. Her hair hung loosely down her back, her jewellery box was untouched and her drawer of scarlet lipsticks, sky-blue eyeshadows and black kohl eyeliner was unopened. Our Mammy seemed to be slipping further away from us with every day that passed.

She was always quiet and even if family came round she wouldn't bother to speak to them, let alone make them a cup of tea. She didn't like us inviting friends round any more and it was such a sad atmosphere that we didn't want to anyway.

If I'd been out, when I walked in the door there would be no smell of stew or steak to greet us.

'Rosie, you make the tea tonight,' Mammy would call from the front room.

'What'll I make, Mammy?'

'Whatever you want,' she'd say. It seemed like she didn't care what we ate. She certainly ate barely anything herself.

And she had no interest in little Danny. I already felt he was my baby. Every time I walked into the room he would start beating his arms up and down whereas he'd scream if Mammy did ever pick him up. He just wasn't used to her holding him.

Every morning I'd get Danny up, change his nappy, dress him and prepare his bottles for the day. Then if I was going into town I'd take him with me or on the occasions that I made it into school, Bridget or one of our older cousins would mind him.

Mammy barely noticed him.

Sometimes Ol'Mammy would come round to try to help Mammy or to attempt to bring her out of herself but she too was lost without Ol'Daddy. They'd been together 40 years and she was struggling to cope with life without him.

With Mammy so low, our house quickly fell into a total tip. With that many kids around the place it went to rack and ruin without Mammy tidying, scrubbing and polishing. The carpets weren't vacuumed and the little bedding plants Mammy had spent so long tending outside found themselves locked in a losing battle with the weeds.

There would be fierce rows between Mammy and Daddy.

'You've got to pull yourself together Theresa,' Daddy

said one day. 'This place looks like a pigsty, and you're no better yourself.'

But Mammy didn't even fight back any more. She just sat there, listening, in a daze.

Infuriated, Daddy yelled at me and Bridget. 'Right, your Mammy's turned into a slob,' he said, 'it's down to you two now to keep this place spick and span.'

Bridget was 15 and had met Dave, her boyfriend, by then though and was always out with him so it fell to me. I was going to school sporadically at that point so not only did I have that and a tiny baby to look after, I also now had a home to keep up and a family to cook for every day. When I was younger I'd dreamed of living an independent life, maybe one day even having a job. I wasn't sure what it would be doing exactly but I was certain it would involve driving my own car, wearing a suit with shoulder pads and getting a pay packet with my name neatly typed on it every week. I'd seen that on the telly and it looked good. How I got to there from where I was I had no idea. I knew instinctively though that no one got a pay packet with their name typed on it if they couldn't read or write. I was still pretty much illiterate due to the chaotic nature of my school attendance. I did want to learn, but by then I was so far behind that the teachers must have just thought I was stupid. And despite all my desire to learn and hope for a different life it was clear that more and more reality – babies, cooking and cleaning – was standing between me and my dream.

I think Mammy's problems were sparked by the shock of losing her father then the trauma of Danny's birth so close to each other. But now I do wonder if, deep down, she'd been unhappy about her marriage for years too and could no longer keep it under wraps. Years afterwards a distant cousin told me that Daddy had had an affair before Mammy became ill and she had never quite got over it. We were kids then so there is no way Mammy would have confided in us and that wasn't the way it worked in traveller families anyway. Affairs were never talked about. In fact, as far as travellers were concerned, they simply didn't happen. I'll never know if it's true but my cousin later told me Mammy had even walked out for a while and left us kids as babies with Daddy. She came back after a few weeks though and I must have been so wee because I have no memory of it myself.

At first we thought Mammy's bad moods would pass and she would slip back into being the way we had always known her.

But something else was also going on that at first we had no idea about. Mammy was drinking. And she was drinking a lot.

7

School Strife

Life at home was pretty miserable in the months after Ol'Daddy died. And with so much to do looking after the house and my younger brothers and sisters, I found it hard to settle in at the local comprehensive we'd joined after returning to Manchester.

But living in a council house meant we were now on the radar of the local council so things like attending school had to be done. While we were on the sites we could pretty much do as we chose about schools, but now our parents would be in trouble if we dodged it.

After leaving Belfast, the sum total of my abilities had been being able to spell 'Station'. On a good day. So by the time I started attending my new school, I was years and years behind all the other kids. I should really have been in with a class of five-year-olds but they left me with teenagers my age, to sink or swim. Of course, I sank. They were reading Macbeth and I was still struggling to write my own name.

To make matters worse I was in school on my own. My younger brothers and sisters were still at primary school and Bridget, Kevin, Marty and Chrissie had been sent together to a different school. 'But why can't I go with them, Mammy?' I'd wail each morning. 'There's 600 country kids in my school and just one traveller – me. I feel like

I've got five heads in there. It's not fair.' I didn't realise then that the older four had been put in a special school for kids with learning disabilities because they were even more behind than me.

It was horrible being all alone in that school and left to listen to the same old insults on my own. 'Oi, Pikey girl,' the older boys would shout. 'D'ya wanna fight?'

I just kept my head down and ignored them. These kids were nothing compared to the children I'd had to face on the school bus in Belfast, but I still hated having to listen to them every day.

Each morning I would cry and beg Daddy to let me off school.

'You've got to go, otherwise we'll have the council round here again,' he'd say. 'Now put your shoes on and get out that door. And just tell those kids, "Sticks and stones will break my bones but words'll never hurt me."'

No sooner had I got into the playground at school then it would all begin. 'Gypsy Girl, you stink.' 'Hey Pikey, are you going to put a spell on me?'

I'd turn and start doing as Daddy had told me. 'Sticks and stones will break . . .' Then I'd think better of it and resort to, 'Just get lost you fat, ugly eedjit.'

That's when they'd start pushing me, pulling my hair or snatching my bag and lobbing it into the bushes.

The bullying at school went on for as long as I was there. Country kids thought a traveller like me was fair game. We did get our own back though because at the end of school me and my classmates would be on the same public bus as Bridget, Kevin, Marty and Chrissie, coming back from their school.

'There he is,' I'd say pointing to whoever had been picking on me that day. Then I'd watch as my brothers piled into them.

After a year, my younger brother Sean joined the school and a year after him came Tommy, so gradually there was some safety in numbers. And as more travellers joined the school they taught us together in a separate classroom. We'd all only been to school for a few weeks here and a few weeks there as we travelled from place to place, so we were so far behind the rest of the kids that I guess we had to be taught separately, otherwise there was just no way we were going to learn anything. But at break time we'd be thrown together with the other kids and still had to cope with the bullying and insults.

When my cousin Lizzie joined the school, she had a terrible time. She wouldn't say boo to a goose so the bullies made her life a total misery. Once, I turned into a corridor and saw her pinned in a corner by the coat hooks, surrounded by a group of girls who were kicking and slapping her as she stood there literally frozen with fear.

I was ready to kill.

'Leave her alone!' I screamed pulling the girls off her and pushing them backwards.

The leader of the gang was this tall black girl. She was about a foot taller than me and I was wheezing as I yanked her hair back and pulled her away from Lizzie.

'Sorry, sorry,' the girl yelped. 'I've seen your brothers fighting on the bus and I don't want trouble.' Then the lot of them ran off. Thanks to my family, I must have had a reputation for being far harder than I actually felt inside.

I looked round at Lizzie in the corner. 'Why didn'tcha hit back, you eedjit?' I said.

Lizzie couldn't stop crying long enough to answer me. I put my arm around her and gave her a hug. 'From now on you stick with me,' I said. 'Don't worry, it'll be OK.'

Although in all honesty I had no confidence that it'd be OK at all. Sometimes life felt like a constant battle: on the way to school, in school, home from school and down our street. There was always someone, somewhere, wanting to fight.

I was sick of it.

Me, Marty, Chrissie and Bridget skipped off school whenever we could get away with it. We'd climb on the bus in the mornings but rather than getting off at our school stop we'd go all the way into town. I'd have slipped a pair of jeans and a sweatshirt into my school bag and change into them in the public toilets at the Arndale Centre. We wandered from shop to shop, played on the escalators and spent three hours sharing a Coke in McDonalds.

The next time I made it into school I'd be handed a letter for my parents, demanding an explanation for my unauthorised absence. When I got home I'd read it to them. 'Rosie was very good today and has no school tomorrow. Please sign below to say you've had this letter.'

'That's grand,' Daddy would say, totally unable to read any different. Then he'd pick up the big black marker pen we kept in the kitchen drawer and make an 'X' at the bottom of the paper.

I hated tricking Daddy but if he found out about the letter he'd have been mad at me, mad at the teachers, mad at everyone and it just wasn't worth the hassle. Daddy was proud of my learning and more than anything I didn't want to disappoint him.

I hated school and was desperate to bunk off whenever I could get away with it, but I did still want to learn. I don't know whether the teachers had low expectations of traveller kids or just couldn't be bothered. Either way, on the days I did make it into school I don't remember doing much else than colouring in.

I wanted to learn, I just didn't know how.

It had never bothered Mammy or Daddy that they couldn't read. If we were ever out looking for a particular road or went to a hospital or a shop, it didn't faze them that they couldn't read signs or directions, they'd just ask whoever was closest to them. I was different though. I was always fascinated by the mysterious looking shapes on road signs and shop windows; I wanted to know what they said.

There was just one teacher at our school in Manchester called Mrs Woods who seemed to understand that although I was still struggling to spell out C-A-T and D-O-G, I did really *want* to learn. She was a good few stone overweight with shiny, black bobbed hair that curved round beneath at least two double chins.

'Don't try and read the whole word at the same time,' she explained to me as I glared angrily at the letters S-H-E and D. Then she covered up the E and D with her chubby finger. 'Just say SH, then look at ED, and you've got SHED. Do you understand?'

'Yes, Miss,' I said. I wasn't totally lying. I did kind of understand but it was to be years before I was actually able to use her advice to begin reading confidently.

Mrs Woods had dozens of other kids to teach, of all

different abilities, so most of the time I was left to copy out long sections from a book, picking up a few words along the way, but mostly not having a clue what I was writing. Then it was back to colouring again. I loved looking at the books though and dreamed of owning my own ones some day.

'When you're out today could you bring me back a book please, Daddy?' I asked one morning.

'Oh, my little professor,' Daddy joked. 'I'll see what I can find.'

It was a couple of days later that Daddy called me over when he pulled up in his truck.

'Look what I've got for you,' he said.

From the deep pocket of his thick, black wool coat, Daddy pulled out a brand-new copy of Roald Dahl's *James and the Giant Peach*. When I opened it, the spine cracked and it smelled of newness.

'Oh Daddy, thank you,' I said. 'Thank you so much.' I felt I could burst with pride.

Mammy thought school and reading and writing was a total waste of time though.

'Reading a book won't get this place cleaned,' she'd say. 'Do you think you're a country girl, sitting there with a book in your hand?'

One afternoon she came home to find the house in a right tip. This was just before Ol'Daddy died when she still gave a toss about how the place looked. I'd been labouring over *James and the Giant Peach* for hours and forgotten all about the beds that needed straightening and the floor that needed mopping.

'I've had enough of this,' Mammy said in a fury as she stomped into the room.

I looked up and could tell immediately that I was in big trouble. I shoved *James and the Giant Peach* under one of the fluffy cushions and darted towards the kitchen, grabbing discarded mugs from the table on my way.

'Sorry, Mammy,' I said. 'I lost track of the time.'

'But that's not good enough,' Mammy yelled back at me. 'You should be helping me. Not wasting your days reading this rubbish.' At that moment she snatched up the cushion and seized my treasured book.

I knew what was coming next.

'It's got to stop,' she said. And then she hurled the book straight into the open coal fire.

'No,' I yelled, already feeling tears choking at the back of my throat. But it was too late. It was all too late. I watched as all those tiny words I'd worked so hard to decipher curled into flakes of black ash. Too angry to cry, I simply walked into the kitchen and started washing the pots.

I never have found out what happens at the end of *James and the Giant Peach*.

Daddy was proud of my reading and writing though and would parade me in front of his friends like a performing seal whenever they came round.

'Rosie, come over here and show your Uncle Paddy how well you can read,' he'd say. I'd then have to pick up a Cornflakes packet or letter from the council and read it out loud. More often than not I hadn't got a clue what it said but I couldn't let Daddy down in public so would come up with something that sounded likely.

Once, he had a copy of a newspaper and asked me to read out the sports pages to the men sitting with him. Very slowly and seriously I read out the headline: 'Ferrari in Pole Position for Grand Pricks.'

Suddenly the men were falling about laughing. I felt myself blushing scarlet. I'd obviously said something very wrong but I didn't have a clue what it was!

'Don't worry, Rosie,' Daddy said, 'that was a good effort, better than this bunch of eedjits here could manage.'

Daddy had an interest in the outside world that Mammy never really shared. He'd come home with newspapers and look at the pictures then ask me to explain what the story was about. Usually I'd only be able to make out a few words, but together we'd work out the rough gist. And travellers from sites all over the city would come round to our house with any official letters they received in the hope I could read them and let them know what all the lines of mysterious type on the page meant.

Daddy was so proud of me. He'd boast to his friends, 'Our Rosie, she's going to be a doctor or a nurse when she gets bigger.' But he was only joking of course. In reality there was no way he would ever consider me being anything other than a wife and mother. In our world women just didn't work outside the home. Sometimes I did dream though of having a proper job.

I loved our life, it was the only life I knew. But I also dreamed of having a different life. I'd lie in bed and think about my future: 'I won't drink, I won't smoke, I won't get married until I'm really old, maybe 30, and I'll have a job, I'll work abroad and fend for myself.' I didn't want my life to be how Mammy's had been before she got sad, a constant round of cleaning, cooking and looking after the children. I wanted to be different. I wanted to be me.

For most girls my age those things wouldn't have been outrageous dreams. But coming from my background, they were. Mammy would have no truck with that kind of thinking. She was a stickler for the 'old ways' of the travellers. She was strict and very traditional. That meant women cleaned and looked good, while men went out to work. Girls didn't need an education to dress up nice and look after the home.

Mammy was also very traditional when it came to us even thinking about relationships with boys. Me and Bridget had it drummed into us from as early as I can remember that we were never to let a boy do so much as kiss us before we were 'going steady'. Not that we had any idea what might happen if we did do something like that – or more. Sex education was firmly off the agenda. Mammy didn't even tell us about periods – and we didn't ever really discuss things that happened 'down there', even between ourselves.

My auntie Chrissie once said to me, 'When you get your yokes, then you're a woman. You'll be an adult.'

I didn't have a clue what she was talking about. 'What's "yokes"?' I said.

'Your time of the month,' she explained slowly.

I was still none the wiser but could see there was little point in asking further.

When I did finally did get my 'yokes' as traveller girls called periods, I was almost 14. I went to the toilet one break time at school, saw blood in my knickers and was convinced I must be dying. At the same time there was a terrible nagging pain in my stomach that wouldn't go away.

'Rosie, do you want to go to see the nurse?' my teacher

asked towards the end of the day. I nodded and trudged off, grasping my aching stomach.

The nurse asked me loads of questions but I wouldn't tell her I was bleeding. Travellers never talked about that sort of thing. In the end she sent me home and told me to get Mammy to call the doctor.

I was lying on the couch in the front room, covered in a quilt, when the doctor turned up. Mammy and Bridget went and waited in another room. The doctor took my temperature and blood pressure, then nodded slowly to himself. 'Rosie,' he said, 'by any chance, are you bleeding?'

'Yes,' I replied, relieved someone had guessed my mystery illness.

'Well why don't you tell your mother this?' he snapped.

'No Sir, I will not,' I replied, still the stroppy teenager. I thought Mammy would kill me if I said such a thing.

The doctor shook his head, zipped up his bag and stomped out the door.

'Well, what did he say? What's wrong with you?' Mammy asked when she came back into the room.

'Dunno,' I said.

I was in and out of the toilet for the rest of the day until our Bridget came up to me with a knowing look and said, 'You've got your yokes on ya, haven't ya.' She handed me an old sheet and told me to tear it into rags and use those every month. 'Here, they're your jam rags. Be sure to burn them in the fire when you've finished.'

So I did as I was told. But I still didn't have the slightest idea what was happening to me and why.

A couple of months later I sat it out when we had a swimming lesson at school.

Our swimming teacher, Miss Davis, was a round-faced woman in her late twenties with long blonde hair that swished from side to side as she walked. She was locked in a constant battle with girls who didn't share her enthusiasm for sport. That was most of us.

'Rosie McKinley,' she shrieked across the swimming pool that morning. 'Why aren't you getting your swimming costume on?'

I felt myself shine scarlet and motioned for her to come closer. She bent down next to me and I whispered in her ear. 'I've got me yokes on me, Miss.'

'Your yokes?' she shrilled at full volume. 'What are you talking about?'

I was mortified. Now everyone in the pool would know it was my yokes. I didn't realise that no one else had a clue what that meant.

She leant forwards again. 'Do you mean your period, Rosie?' she asked.

'Period?' I shouted back above the noise of the pool, so everyone turned to stare at me. 'No, I don't know what that is, Miss.'

There was an outbreak of sniggering. My face burned crimson. The only periods I knew about were things like Maths Period, or Double History Periods. Afterwards when I realised what I'd yelled out across the pool, I was crying with shame. I really was clueless.

Mammy didn't talk about anything like that. By then she was seriously low and not talking about anything much but even before then she would never discuss anything she referred to as 'private matters'. Even though the babies kept appearing in our trailer year after year, there was never any discussion about where they might have come from. Most of the time we knew better than to ask, but one time when Mammy was tired and crotchety and soon to give birth for the sixth or seventh time, I could contain my curiosity no longer. 'But where do babies come out?' I kept asking her, over and over, all day long.

'Out ya hole,' she finally snapped back. She must have run right out of patience with me to say something like that.

But what could that mean? I wondered. Your earhole, or nostril? Finally I worked it out. 'She must mean your mouth,' I thought to myself. I stood in front of the mirror in Mammy's bedroom, opening my mouth as wide as I could. Hmmm, it didn't look very big for a baby to come out of. Surely, you'd choke. When the baby finally arrived I'd spend ages looking at his head wondering how on earth that had come out of Mammy's mouth. But I never plucked up the courage to ask Mammy about it again.

Thankfully I had no plans for getting married or having babies myself for quite some time. I'd had enough looking after the little'uns at home. And of course, Mammy had brought us up real strict. 'You never let a boy touch your skin till you're married,' she'd say. And we weren't allowed to drink and smoke until we were married either.

When I was about 14, I was allowed to start going to some of the discos that were organised by traveller families for their teenage kids in halls all over the north of England. It was often hard for traveller kids to get into discos run by country people because of the discrimination against us, so we had our own do's instead.

Me and Bridget would spend all week planning what we

were going to wear. My hair was in a long flick then with blonde highlights that me and Bridget had spent hours toiling over with a home hair-dye kit from Superdrug. I thought the whole effect was very Princess Diana although it is possible I looked more like a badger with bleached blonde patches in my black hair.

Marty and Kevin almost always came with me, Bridget and Chrissie to the discos. And us three girls would probably have had more leniency if we'd been out with Mother Theresa. No sooner had a boy come up to the three of us than Kevin and Marty would be by our sides bogging this poor kid out. If they knew his family and thought he was alright, he'd be allowed to stop and chat, at least for a while. But if they didn't like the look of him they soon made it known. 'You feckin' lay a finger on one of them girls and we'll beat your brains out,' they'd say.

Country girls would probably have hated a brother acting like that. But us traveller girls knew our reputation was everything. If we were thought to be flirting or hanging around a boy who was no good, it could get us tainted for life.

I was learning quickly that there were massive double standards going on. Girls had to be whiter than white at all times while boys were trying to chat up anything that moved. Back then, I didn't question it though. Again, it was just the way things were.

I was still a tomboy at heart with little interest in 'going steady' with anyone, but there was one boy I did fancy. His name was Brian Milligan and he got a grudging seal of approval from Kevin and Marty. I think his family were cousins with our family, way back in time and he had a reputation as a good, honest lad. At one of the discos he asked me out and even though dating only meant weekly trips to the cinema or ice rink with our friends as chaperones, I still thought that was really cool. He had close-cropped black hair and a tooth missing at the front. He was no Rick Astley, but he had a twinkle in his eye and was dead funny. Every girl around was mental about him, but I had him. We went together for about three months but it was all entirely innocent. Daddy didn't know though. He would have thought I was far too young for boys and would have given out awful bad.

Me and Brian would meet up in town on a Saturday with a gang of others and sometimes he'd come round to see my brother Kevin. Brian wouldn't have dared to do anything more than hold my hand. He didn't even think about touching me beyond that. He'd have got a kick in the face off me, before Marty and Kevin had even started on him.

We'd been together a couple of months when a friend of mine took me to one side at a disco.

'Hey, Rosie, my cousin saw your Brian out on his own with a blonde girl in town at the weekend. I just thought you ought to know.'

When I saw Brian the next night and asked him what had happened, he seemed vague. 'When?' he said.

'Last weekend.'

'Oh, where?'

'Down the town.'

'Oh, I'm not sure,' he said.

'Well, it's not difficult,' I snapped. 'You've either been out with someone else or you haven't.'

'Er, no, no I haven't,' he said.

I thought he was lovely, so I didn't ask any more questions. I just wanted to believe Brian liked me as much as I liked him. But it was only a fortnight later that another mate told me she'd seen him at a disco with a red-haired girl. Then the following week it turned out he was at the cinema with a third girl. I'd had enough.

At the next Friday night disco I felt physically sick waiting for him to walk in the door. Part of me desperately wanted to see him but another part never wanted to clap eyes on him again.

'Alright, Rosie?' said Brian, wandering over with his hands thrust into his jeans pockets.

'Hi,' I said quietly. The only thing going through my mind were the words, 'Don't cry. Don't cry. Don't cry. Whatever he says, don't cry.'

'I keep hearing stories about you,' I said.

'Oh yeah,' he said, smirking. 'All good I take it?'

Suddenly I was angry. I felt a new strength building up inside me. 'No, not really,' I said. 'Not at all. In fact, you can piss right off.'

The smile slid off his face and I stomped off, still frantically repeating 'Don't cry, Don't cry' under my breath. And I pretty much managed it all the way to the ladies' loos, where I collapsed in a blubbering heap. But at least I'd showed that, at 14, I was a young woman not to be messed with. If only I'd stayed so strong with men as I got older.

8

Out to Work

'Daddy, why can't girls work?' I asked one evening after putting the little'uns to bed and picking up their toys from the front room floor.

'Because there's enough work for a woman looking after the children,' Daddy replied. 'It's a man's place to provide – it's what he is supposed to do. A wife is supposed to look after the children.'

My sister Bridget had just married her boyfriend Dave, who came from a good traveller family that Daddy had known for years. She was only 17, but that was regarded as just the right age for marriage in our culture. Hardly any traveller girls were still single at 20 and after that they'd be considered 'over the hill'.

On the morning of the wedding, I helped Bridget into her simple, white A-line dress. She looked barely different to the day she'd taken her First Holy Communion, aged eight. She was frighteningly young. Maybe what was most frightening was that I knew I was just two years behind her and soon it would be me standing where she was.

'You look lovely, B,' I told her.

'Thanks, Rosie.'

'Are you OK about it all then?' I asked.

'What d'you mean?' she said.

'Y'know, getting married, being a wife, all of that.'

Maybe I meant sex, which I was now dimly aware of. But I meant all the rest of it too – looking after a fella, having kids, getting old. The whole thing was pretty scary. As she stood at the altar in St Peter's Church near our house, I was thinking she looked just as young and scared as when we used to be out playing Knockalash in the street. And here she was getting married.

It was a quiet little wedding by traveller standards because with Mammy still not back to her old self, things weren't the same in our family. But there were still probably more than 100 people there for the service and a big party afterwards in a hall at the side of the church.

Bridget and Dave moved into a council flat down the road from us, which meant caring for the house and the little'uns was entirely my job. Kevin was out working with Daddy and in traveller world, if a mammy couldn't care for the family then it was down to the daughters.

So that day as I talked with Daddy about my future, it didn't sound very appealing to me at all. I was already looking after a home and kids – I didn't fancy doing it for the rest of my life! But what else, as a gypsy girl, could I really do?

I'd been attending school less and less and I didn't stand a hope in hell of passing any exams. Soon after the conversation with Daddy, a careers teacher from the education authority came to the house, obviously intent on finding me something meaningful to do with my life.

'Now, Rosie,' said the careers teacher, 'we need to find you a job.'

'No, no, no,' said Daddy who was sitting in the corner of the room, glaring at the woman in the navy suit and off-white polyester-mix shirt. 'She don't need no job. Her mammy needs her here to look after the little'uns.'

'But I want to go to work, Daddy,' I joined in. 'Why shouldn't I?'

Things became a little heated. Daddy sat in the corner growling about how a good traveller woman should be at home, bringing up the kids well and looking after her man. But the careers officer, all credit to her, just gave him a polite nod then carried on yacking about training programmes, apprenticeships and work placements. Some people might have been intimidated by my hulking father, but not this lady.

'So what are you good at, Rosie?' the careers lady breezed on regardless.

'Nothin' much,' I said.

'She's good at looking after her family,' Daddy yelled across.

'He's right,' I said. 'The only things I can really do are look after kids and cook.'

'Excellent,' she replied. 'If you can cook, how about a job as a trainee chef?'

Now that sounded good.

'Yes,' I said.

'No,' said Daddy, a split second later.

But it was too late. I'd set my heart on it and spent the following week begging, cajoling and doing deals with Daddy to let me at least try the job out. I wanted to earn my own money and learn something new. By then I was caring for the younger kids almost all of the time, but I was sure I could do both. And it would be a break from the drudgery of life at home.

Two weeks later I started work in the restaurant of a

hotel a couple of miles from where we lived. Mammy was past caring what I did and Daddy had grudgingly agreed in the end so long as Bridget could come round and help out with the little'uns when I wasn't there. I think he thought it'd be a novelty for me and I'd have packed it in within the week. But he couldn't have been more wrong. I loved turning up to work every day at the same time as all the managers in their dark suits and seeing the tourists with their expensive suitcases and designer clothes.

The head chef was a short, stumpy woman with greying curls that burst out the side of her chef's hat. Her name was Stella and I could tell by the way she looked me up and down on my first morning that she had already been told I was a traveller. She was probably furious that I'd been foisted on her. When she gave me a half-hour lecture on cleanliness I was certain she knew about my background. Most country people assume travellers are dirty.

Once Stella had finished her lecture, she stood back and watched as I cleaned down the work surfaces, under her supervision. But no one had been a better trainer in cleanliness than Mammy back before Ol'Daddy had died. You could eat your dinner off our kitchen floor in those days. I sprayed the surfaces with cleaner then, using scalding hot water, I scrubbed the worktops until no germ could possibly have survived.

'Jesus,' Stella said afterwards. 'I've never seen anyone scrub so hard and so quickly.'

Then she gave me the carrots and beans to prepare for lunch. Ten minutes later I went over to where she was standing at the hot plate, to tell her I'd finished.

'I need you to do the whole lot in the box,' she snapped.

'I have,' I replied, shaking the empty container.

'Oh,' she said, finally smiling at me. 'I see you're going to be good.'

I concentrated hard on my chopping board so she wouldn't see my face burning red with pride. No one had ever said I was good at anything before. It was the best feeling in the world.

She'd obviously thought I'd be slow and dirty and cloddy – which is a traveller word for useless – but once she realised I could do the job, she treated me with a new respect. And I loved learning from her everything she could teach me about food. Within two months I had been promoted from food preparation to the dessert counter and from there on to the hot plate where all the main meals were cooked.

I'd never spent so much time with country people but we all got on great. We were mates.

Daddy still hated me working and I got a lot of slagging from the other travellers too. I'd have to go to work every day in my white overalls and white tights, carrying my white hat in my hand. If any of the travellers who lived near us saw me, they'd start yelling out in the street. 'Oooh, look at her, thinks she's a right country girl now, she does,' they'd shout.

'Shut it you eedjits,' I'd yell back over my shoulder, walking away as quickly as I could.

One lunchtime I'd just finished serving up some beef bourgignon when I heard a commotion at the side of the restaurant. I looked over and saw a group of about ten traveller men walking towards me. I knew them all, and I could tell they were here to cause trouble. They were rubbing

their hands together and smacking their lips in a ridiculous, over-the-top way.

'So, Mikey, what'll we have from this delicious menu?' I
heard one of the lads called Jerry say.

I felt sick. They were about to ruin everything I'd
worked for.

'Slap some of that beef on here, Rosie,' Jerry said. 'And
you'll see us alright won't you?'

That was traveller talk for meaning they had no intention of paying.

'No,' I said. 'I can't do that, and I won't.'

'Oh yes you can, Rosie,' he replied. He was trying to
threaten me. This was how these fellas acted all the time,
intimidating people rather than paying for anything fair
and square. But I was sick of being bullied by country
people – I certainly wasn't going to have it from gypsies as
well. Their behaviour was putting at risk the job I loved
and that made me furious. Suddenly I was more angry at
them than I was frightened about causing a scene. I went
back into the kitchens and told Stella, the head chef, what
was going on. 'They want me to give them it all for free,' I
said. 'But I won't do it.'

She was brilliant and within minutes, two security officers were escorting the travellers quietly off the premises. I
didn't make myself popular and the next time I saw those
lads they were yelling and calling me all the names under
the sun, but quite frankly, I didn't give a toss.

I was respected at work, I was earning my own wage and
was able to treat Danny with sweets and toys. Thursday
was pay day and it was all cash in hand, so the minute I
took off my apron I'd be out the door and down to Woolies

in the shopping centre to find something for little Danny. At the time he loved Thomas the Tank Engine on the telly and so over a few months I treated him to every engine in Sodor! When I could afford it I'd get little treats for the other kiddies too but Danny was special to me. In many ways he felt more like my little boy than Mammy's. She'd shown barely a flicker of interest in him since the day he was born. And since he didn't get any treats from Mammy and Daddy, I wanted to feel I was doing something to make things better for him. I kept a few quid in case I wanted to go into town with my mates at the weekend and the rest of it I handed over to Mammy and Daddy for my keep – that was the traveller way.

Working made me feel like a proper woman. Life was hard though. Mammy was still lost in her own world and had never gone back to looking after the kids and the house.

Some days she didn't even get out of bed. When she did she would be sitting on the sofa when I left for work in the morning and still be there when I returned at night. Before Ol'Daddy died, her naturally dark hair would change colour practically with the weather, thanks to the Clairol home hair-dye kits she kept stashed in the bathroom cabinet. One week it would be honey blonde, the next she would have switched to aubergine red, and the following week she would have plumped for ebony black. But now she had long grey roots of wiry hair with the remnants of her last hair dye experiment down below her ears.

Deep wrinkles had cut themselves into her skin and her eyes were lifeless. Most of the time she couldn't or wouldn't focus on whoever was in the room when they tried to talk to her. The dressing table where Mammy had once sat for hours 'doing herself up' was now thick with dust.

At the hotel, I was normally on lunch duty, which meant I had to be up at five o'clock every morning to be in work at just after six.

I'd lay out all the kids' school clothes the night before, then in the morning I'd get them up and dressed, give them their breakfast and make sure they were ready for school. Then I could just leave them in front of the telly when I ran out of the door so as not to be late for work. It was a terrible early start for the kids but it was the only way I could be sure they'd get their uniforms on and have a decent meal inside them before leaving the house.

Daddy gave me the housekeeping money so that on the way home from work I could go to the shops and buy some food. Then when I got back I'd cook the tea, then do the washing up, clean the house, put the washing on and get the kids to bed again. On top of that I was also having to do Danny's physiotheraphy exercises with him twice a day as his limbs were still floppy and he was slow in learning to walk. The condition he'd been born with had left him with mobility difficulties but the doctors were confident that with regular physio he should make good improvements.

One day, some of Mammy's cousins came round to visit her. I was bringing them in a pot of tea and some biscuits when Mammy looked up at me and laughed. 'Look, here's Tommy's wife,' she said. 'Rosie's the wife round here now. She does everything. I could be dead and buried and no one would notice any more.'

'Mammy,' I said. 'God forgive you.' I was mortified that

she would say such a thing in front of other people and would also let them know what a state she was in. But she didn't care what she said any more.

For months we'd been hoping that Mammy would just snap out of her low mood but we had to face the reality that it might never happen. Finally, Daddy and me took her to the doctor and told him everything that had happened since Ol'Daddy's death. Then we were sent out to the waiting room while the doctor spoke to Mammy on her own. When she emerged she was holding a prescription. I'm not even sure whether she ever took the medication though. Her mood certainly didn't change one bit.

It may have been partly because I was so sick of everything going on at home that around then I started going out with a distant cousin of mine called Tony. We'd meet at family parties and get-togethers and one day he asked me out to the cinema with him and a group of his mates. Still as a traveller girl I wouldn't go anywhere on my own with a boyfriend. I didn't really have time for a proper relationship what with work and the kids to look after. But I'd see him occasionally on a Saturday afternoon when a group of us would go ice skating or wander round the town together. Mammy was way beyond caring where I went or who it was with. And I didn't tell Daddy. Although he thought I was old enough to look after the whole family and was just about coming to terms with the idea that I had a job, he'd have still thought me too young to have a boyfriend.

In reality it wasn't really a boyfriend/girlfriend thing, it was just that if we saw each other we did, and if we didn't, we didn't. We were more like friends than anything else. I may have been sixteen but I was still as innocent as a ten-year-old.

Mammy spent almost every day in her bedroom with the curtains closed and the door firmly shut. If me or any of the little'uns knocked, she'd shout, 'Leave me alone.'

Sometimes I'd take her up a sandwich and a cup of tea but when I went back hours later they would still be lying untouched by the side of the bed. The little'uns couldn't really understand what was going on so they just stuck with me.

One afternoon I was late home from work and I didn't have time to tidy up the house and cook the tea before Daddy came in. He walked around the house, looking at the piles of toys, dirty clothes and general chaos. The fire was unlit and there was a pile of free newspapers and junk mail lining the hall carpet. Then he went into the kitchen. There was no food in the cupboards and no dinner on the hob.

For months I'd managed to hide from him just how little Mammy had been doing, but that day I think he realised.

'Theresa, come down here this minute,' Daddy shouted up the stairs. 'This place is a tip and you lying there all day in your pit. You're a disgrace.'

There was no movement from upstairs.

'Come out of that bedroom,' Daddy shouted again.

Still nothing. I could tell he was getting really mad now but I didn't think that was enough to get Mammy out of bed.

'Get down here now,' he yelled.

Finally, after about ten minutes, Mammy trudged down

the stairs, her pale blue towelling dressing gown hanging open, and her hair greasy and lank.

'I've had enough of this,' Daddy was yelling. 'You're a tramp. From tomorrow you're going to get up off your arse and wash yourself and then you're going to clean this house up.'

Mammy started screaming back at him. 'The only reason I'm this way is because you made me like it.' After months of barely speaking, it was as if he'd ignited something inside her and now she wasn't going to stop.

Then she turned to me and the little'uns who were all crowded together on the sofa. 'You think your daddy's so great, doncha?' she said. 'But he's why I'm like this. He's a bad man. He's going with a girl. Oh yes, he's got his own whore and she's going to give you a wee brother or sister.'

'You're crazy, Theresa,' Daddy screeched back.

The whole thing was so horrible and so frightening for the little'uns that I didn't really take in exactly what Mammy was saying. I certainly didn't for one moment think there might be any truth in it. I pushed the kids upstairs to bed and left Mammy and Daddy screaming at each other in the lounge.

A few days later I was standing in the kitchen when I saw Mammy go out into the garden. She seemed a bit calmer and I thought maybe finally she'd got her anger out of her system and she was on the mend. I was delighted to see her in the garden because I thought maybe she was regaining interest in all the plants she had bedded out before Ol'Daddy died.

She was kneeling on the grass holding a trowel but her back was to me and I couldn't see what she was doing. She was there for ages and when she finally finished and returned upstairs I went outside to see what she had been working on. But when I got out there, all the weeds were still intact.

Then I noticed that a patch of grass on the lawn seemed to have been dug away and replaced. I picked up the clod of earth and suddenly everything that had been going on for months became crystal clear. In the ground, squeezed between two old bricks, was an empty bottle of Smirnoff vodka.

'So that's it,' I said quietly. 'Oh Mammy.'

I walked slowly around the garden and found another patch that had been recently dug up. Again I kicked the grass away, and this time I found two half-empty bottles.

'How much more of this is there?' I thought.

I went over to the grey plastic shed in the corner of the garden where Mammy kept her trowel, rake and spade. Inside under an old, plastic compost bag there was a pile three feet high of crushed-down beer cans and empty vodka bottles. There were literally dozens of bottles – litres and litres of vodka.

I rang Bridget and told her what I'd found.

'Oh Jesus,' she said quietly. 'I'll be round in five minutes.'

As soon as she arrived we went from room to room, searching for clues as to what Mammy had been doing.

There had been a creaky floorboard in the bathroom for years but now when I looked closely I saw that it had been lifted up. Using a back scrubber from the cupboard, I wedged the board up again – underneath it was littered with more cans and bottles.

As we walked around the house we found them

everywhere; in the space under the kitchen cupboards, in a false floor in the airing cupboard, even crammed inside the blocked-up chimney breasts.

The more I thought, the more I realised how utterly stupid I'd been to not see the signs that Mammy had been drinking heavily ever since Ol'Daddy's death. All those times she wouldn't let us into her room and all the mornings when she'd been unable to get out of bed. But I'd always thought people who were drunk would be rolling around on the floor or slurring their words and Mammy had never been like that. She'd just been quiet and withdrawn.

Before Ol'Daddy died Mammy would go to the pub on a Sunday afternoon with Daddy but after two vodka and Cokes she'd always say, 'That's my lot.' This was in a different league.

I didn't dare ask Daddy if he knew what was going on but instinctively I realised that he must have done. The rows between them had been getting worse and worse. Now I realised what he'd been talking about when he yelled at her to pull herself together.

But I still couldn't bring myself to confront Mammy with what we'd found. It felt like talking about it would make it real. I didn't know what to do or who to confide in. All I could do was pray every night that things might go back to the way they once were. But by then I was praying for a miracle.

9

Goodbye to Our Mammy

Over the next year Mammy just became worse and worse. Soon she was sleeping all night in her clothes and wouldn't change them at all until Bridget and I went in there and peeled them off her to put them in the washing machine. Her bedroom smelt of decay and neglect. Then she started peeing herself in the night. I'd go in to check on her in the morning and be hit by the stench of urine. I'd lift her out of the bed then change the sheets before laying her back down again. But the next night the same thing would happen and I'd be changing the sheets and washing them again before going to work.

As the months went by it became blindingly obvious she was drinking even though she was still incredibly secretive about it. Despite regular sweeps of the house, I still rarely found her stashes of booze until the bottles and cans were empty.

Daddy had been furious at Mammy for months on end. But then it was almost like he gave up on her and just distanced himself from what was going on. He'd moved into a box room in the house and came and went as he pleased. It was strange behaviour but at the time I thought he was just trying to pretend it wasn't happening. Somehow I still managed to hold down my job as well as look after the kids, and, thank God, Bridget was always round at ours helping out.

At one point things were so bad that Daddy took Mammy back to the doctor and told him about the drinking. But if she didn't want to stop, there was little the GP could do.

'Mrs McKinley, if you want to be able to look after your children and see them grow up you have got to stop drinking,' the doctor said.

But Mammy no longer cared about looking after her children. The only thing she cared about was drink.

Then Daddy took her to the priest. 'Father, you've got to help us,' he pleaded. 'My wife is killing herself.'

The priest prayed with Mammy and Daddy and told them he'd always be there for support, but there was nothing he could really do either.

'Please stop drinking, Mammy,' I'd say. 'Little Danny needs you, he's still very poorly. We all need you.'

But it was too late.

'I'll drink till I die,' she'd reply. I reckon she just wanted to be with Ol' Daddy.

Sometimes I'd try to remind her of the old days. How she'd dress up in her Alexis Colby power suits and go out dancing with Daddy. But that just seemed to make her sadder. It was as if all that had happened to her in another life, one that she was barred from returning to. Then other times I'd just get angry with her for choosing drink over her family. 'Daddy's right,' I'd scream. 'You're just a lazy, selfish tramp.' But that made no difference either.

She started lying more and more. Sometimes I'd cook her a fry-up for breakfast and then a sandwich for lunch and take it up to her room where she would pick at it for a while. But if one of her cousins or friends came around to visit her later, she'd say, 'I haven't had a thing to eat all day. Nor a cup of tea or a sip of water and I'm gasping. They don't do nothing for me here y'know.' Then I'd get an ear bashing from the cousin on their way out. 'I can't believe you would treat your Mammy so bad, not even making her a wee sandwich when she's up in that room on her own, day after day. Make her a cup of tea this minute, Rosie.'

She'd never been a cuddly mum. Not one for hugs and kisses, but she was always there looking after us and making sure everything we needed was sorted when we were little. Now she was going I felt angry at Mammy and Daddy. The little'uns had been caught in the middle of rows for years and now neither Mammy or Daddy seemed interested in them at all anymore. It seemed like neither of them could think of anyone but themselves.

One night I'd just got the little'uns bathed, in their pyjamas and into bed when Mammy screeched at us from downstairs. 'Come down here all of ya, right now,' she yelled. We all trooped down, nervously. I was holding little Danny on my hip. He was still just a toddler so thank God he had no idea what was going on. Daddy was sat in an armchair in the corner, Mammy was laid out on the couch.

'Me and your Daddy are getting divorced,' she said. 'Now, each of ya, who d'ya want to live with?'

'You can't ask that, Mammy,' I said.

'You shut it,' she yelled back. 'We know you'll be going with your Daddy to do his cooking and ironing. You think he's so great,' she slurred. 'But he's the one that's been carrying on with some whore who's carrying his baby.' She was back onto this subject again but still I was convinced it was just her drunken ramblings.

'Daddy wouldn't do that,' I shouted at her. 'You've drunk so much you don't know what you're talking about.'

My little sisters Tina and Maria were already in tears so I pushed them back out of the doorway. I was furious that their childhood was being destroyed.

When Mammy eventually went up to bed, I turned to Daddy. 'She is lying, isn't she?' I asked him. Deep down, something was worrying me. Was there any chance that Mammy was actually telling the truth?

'I am not having an affair,' Daddy said, leaning over and kissing the top of my head. 'Now get off to bed.'

I lay down that night, relieved. Daddy wasn't having an affair. He'd told me. And he wouldn't lie. Not to me. But still, Daddy was spending less and less time at home. I thought he must be finding the atmosphere as unbearable as the rest of us and going off to the pub every night to escape it. Most nights now he'd bolt his tea down then get himself all smartened up to go down the pub. It was odd that just at the time Mammy had lost all interest in her appearance, he was making a real effort. I'd normally be asleep by the time Daddy got home.

Daddy was rarely around to talk to the little 'uns and I'd had enough of the way they were being treated by their Mammy and Daddy. After weeks of worrying and thinking about it I came up with a plan. I decided it was up to me to give my little brothers and sisters a better life. I decided to run away with them.

I had it all worked out. I'd get their things together then go and stay with our cousin Susan until we were able to find a place of our own far away from Mammy and Daddy. I'd spoken to Susan about it on the phone and she'd said it'd be fine so long as we didn't stop long. I had wild hopes that we'd only be there a week at most before I'd be able to find us a permanent flat and maybe a job as a chef that would earn enough to support the lot of us.

I'd lie awake at night working out my plan. How I'd get us all away, what I'd need to take and how much I'd need to earn. I was worried Daddy would go mad and bring us all back when he found we'd gone. But I thought most likely neither him nor Mammy would even be that bothered.

One night I packed two bags with just a few clothes and belongings that we needed, then rang my cousin Susan saying we were ready to leave. But the moment she answered the phone I could tell by her umming and ahhing that something had changed.

'Oh, I'm sorry Rosie, but I told my husband and he said you can't come. Your Daddy will go mad if you run away, he'll lose all face among his friends and then he'd take it out on us. My husband says we just can't go against him.'

I put the phone down and started to cry. Maybe deep down I'd always known it was a silly, childish plan. How on earth would I have been able to look after seven children on my own? And Daddy would always have come to get us and all I'd have done was upset the kids even more, taking them from home to God knows where.

So we stayed put and things dragged on the same.

At night I'd put the kids to bed and stroke their heads until they fell asleep.

Mammy was doing nothing to keep herself clean any more and it was up to Bridget and me to wash her.

One day Bridget came round and we lifted Mammy out of bed, carried her into the bathroom, undressed her then bathed her.

'Stop it, stop it,' she was screaming. 'I don't need a bath and I'm not getting washed.'

'Yes, y'are,' I said, yanking her top off and forcing her into the water.

This was from a woman who'd not that long ago had a collection of cosmetics and lotions like you saw in the perfume counter of a fancy department store. Chanel, Estee Lauder and Elizabeth Arden had all lined her dressing table in a perfect row. Now she was filthy. It was heart-breaking.

Finally Mammy sat in the bath and I sponged her down and washed her hair while Bridget went back into the bedroom and changed the bed.

As time went on I became convinced Daddy was having an affair. The signs were certainly all there: the way he showered, put on a clean shirt, splashed on aftershave and buffed up his shoes now before going down the pub in the evening. When had he ever done that before? And there were the times I woke in the middle of the night and realised that he still wasn't in, long after closing time.

But I idolised my Daddy and in the travellers' culture, affairs were utterly shameful. Cheating carried a far greater stigma than it did for country people. To us it seemed like all country people cheated and lied on their husbands and wives all the time. And everything we watched on television only convinced us of that. We'd grown up with a far stronger moral code than country people. Family was the cornerstone of our lives and having an affair and destroying your family was about the worst thing a man could do. But I was having to face the fact that no matter what I'd thought the rules were, people in our culture were now breaking them. I was determined to find out once and for all what was going on and started watching him like a hawk.

Around that time the GP suggested Mammy should go into hospital for a while.

'Maybe we can give her a few weeks to dry out and keep her in a place where no one will be able to smuggle in alcohol,' our GP suggested. 'Because if we don't stop her drinking soon she will kill herself,' he went on.

We agreed, and Mammy was carted off to a special unit for people suffering from addictions.

With her in hospital Daddy would bolt his dinner down in the evenings and say he was rushing out to visit Mammy. I wasn't convinced. I watched him every time he left the house. Sometimes he did go off in his car in the direction of the hospital but other times he went straight down the road to the local pub. One night I decided to follow him. I waited until he'd been gone an hour or so then walked down to the pub myself. The building had a window quite high up at the front that looked straight down into the lounge bar. I could still climb as well as any boy and I worked out a way of stretching my fingers over the windowsill then hoisted myself up until my whole body was crouched on the ledge. Most of the window panes were frosted glass, which made it impossible to see through, but one had been replaced with clear glass, which meant I had a perfect view into the bar.

And there was Daddy inside the pub, with *her*. She had blonde highlighted hair and white jeans that were so tight you could see her knicker line. I knew instantly she was a country woman. Don't ask me how, but travellers can spot country people at a hundred yards. And I'd never seen her in my life before. If she had been a traveller living in that area I would have known everything about her.

But the worst bit of all was that she looked barely older than me. They were sat at a corner table, chatting. It felt so strange because everything about Daddy was totally familiar to me; the dark hairs that poked out the bottom of his shirt cuff, the way he pinched his cigarette between his thumb and his first finger for the last few drags and how he leaned back slightly whenever he laughed. But at the same time everything about Daddy was now utterly unfamiliar. The man holding hands with a brassy bit barely out of her teens in the middle of a pub was like a total stranger to me.

I couldn't understand how the family I'd thought was so perfect was falling apart in such a terrible way. I was shell-shocked. I needed someone to blame – and that became *her*.

I didn't challenge Daddy that first night. I'm not sure why, maybe I was frightened about how he would react. So instead, every evening after he went out I'd walk to the pub and spy on him. I did it for weeks. Most nights he'd be there with her, drinking and laughing at the same table.

Sometimes I'd see other traveller men with women who clearly weren't their wives either. It hit me like a bolt of lightning that everything I'd believed about men keeping their marriage vows for life was just a heap of crap. The

way things were looking, men were having affairs whenever
and wherever they could.

I think travellers were about 20 years behind country
people when it comes to affairs and divorce. For years and
years it was a very shameful thing for everyone in this country but gradually it became the norm, and I guess it had
started happening more and more among travellers too; it
was just that it took me a while to cotton on to it.

After a few weeks Mammy was discharged from hospital,
but rather than get better her condition just spiralled down-
wards. Me and Bridget were working so hard at preventing
anyone from bringing any alcohol near her but the minute
our backs were turned she would be out the front door and
off to buy it herself. Sometimes she didn't come home all
day. Other times she was gone for a couple of nights. Me and
Bridget would walk the streets for miles around looking for
her, asking in off-licences and visiting cousins in case she
had turned up at theirs begging for a drink.

We'd sit at home sick with worry until time and again a
police car would pull up outside and an officer would pull
Mammy out of the back seat covered in filth. Other times
we'd be called to the hospital or police station to pick her
up because she would have been found down the town,
totally obliterated.

Everything at home was utterly miserable. Work was the
only thing that kept me going. At least when I was there I
couldn't be worrying about Mammy's drinking, Daddy's
affair and all the things I needed to do to keep the little'uns
fed, watered and clothed.

I was still going out with my cousin Tony in our very
innocent way. That went on for a couple of years but it was

never anything serious and we often didn't see each other for months on end.

Then one night at one of the travellers' discos, one of my cousins called Mary said her boyfriend's best mate, Stevie, really wanted to go out with me.

'Whatever,' I replied. I was pretty cool about boys and although I'd seen Stevie around and he was a good-looking lad, he seemed a bit rough to me.

Stevie was a traveller too and his parents spent a lot of time moving between the north of England and Cornwall. A month or so later his family moved to a site near our house and started hanging around with me and my cousins.

'Will ya go out with me, Rosie?' Stevie whispered to me one evening as we were sat sharing a milkshake between five of us in McDonalds.

'I don't think so,' I said, shaking my head. He was one of those lads that had trouble written all over him and the last thing I needed right then was more trouble.

Over the next few days he kept asking and asking but I still said no. He was well over 6ft tall and was a stocky lad with bushy brown hair and eyebrows so thick they met in the middle. His family were good people but I knew that he'd been in fights with other traveller boys and had a reputation for finding trouble wherever he could.

One evening a group of us were round at my cousin Mary's trailer when Stevie walked over to where I was sitting, picked me up, pushed me against the wall and tried to kiss me. I pushed him away. 'What the feck d'ya think you're doing?' I said. 'Just trying,' he laughed. He plonked me back down again then walked out the door.

It might not have been that subtle. But it worked.

I knew then that I liked him, although I still didn't want him to know that!

'Will ya go to the pictures with me?' he asked a few days later.

'I can't, I've got to mind my brothers and sisters,' I said.

But he wouldn't take no for an answer and every day for the next fortnight he asked again. Finally I agreed and we trooped off together to the Odeon in town. But all the films had started by the time we got there and we ended up sharing a pizza instead. We had a laugh but it was nothing serious. Not then. Sometimes we'd go out in a big group down the park or into town. His best pal was a lad called Shane and he was going out with my cousin Mary who lived in a trailer site ten minutes from our house so the four of us were together all the time.

At the end of an evening Stevie would walk me home. When we got there we'd stand on our front step for ages talking about this, that and a whole lot of nothing really. But to be honest by then all I'd be able to think about was the moment when Stevie would lean down and try to kiss me. He was big and strong and his lips were quite rough so that when he kissed me it was like being hit by a bus. But it was brilliant too. I could feel myself falling for Stevie but there was no way I'd ever do more than have a kiss and a cuddle with him. That was absolutely as far as it went. In our culture, sex before marriage was an absolute no-no and Stevie wouldn't even have considered trying his luck in that department!

One night though Daddy came back from the pub and found us snogging on the doorstep. He'd had a few pints and was raging. He pulled Stevie off me and flung him down the garden path while yanking me inside the front door.

'Rosie, I don't want to see him in here or around here or anywhere near you ever again,' he shouted at me. 'That boy is trouble – I've seen his sort a million times before. You'll not see him again. Do you understand?'

'Yes, Daddy,' I said. I'd no intention of keeping my promise though. After all, I thought, Daddy was doing whatever he wanted these days, why on earth shouldn't I? The very next day me and Stevie were out down the town again, hanging round the shops and having marathon snogging sessions down the side of the High Tide chippie.

Stevie had a silly streak to him and was great fun to be around. One afternoon we ran through the arcade singing 'Agadoo' at the tops of our voices while all the shoppers looked at us as if we were total loonies.

Another day, he sat me down in a café and told me he had something important to say.

'I've saved all my money and got you a diamond ring,' Stevie said in a really serious voice.

'Oh, right,' I said, opening the Swan Vesta matchbox he'd pulled out of the front pocket of his jeans. I picked up the huge stone and slipped it on my finger.

'Hey, this would have cost you a fortune,' I said. 'If you hadn't got it out of a cracker last Christmas!'

I threw the matchbox at him pretending to be outraged. Then we started wrestling before collapsing into giggles. That was Stevie's idea of a great joke. He was just a bit crazy. I loved being with him. When we were together I didn't have to worry about home and everyone else. It was just me and Stevie, having a laugh.

In traveller culture if you go steady with a boy for a couple of weeks then people expect you to be thinking about getting married. But I had no intention of doing that, I was still a kid and just having fun. I had no intention of winding up like Mammy, cooking, cleaning and caring for babies all day every day until it sent me clean mad from the drudgey of it all.

But within a few weeks my plans and dreams for the future were to be dealt a massive blow.

10

Runaways

One evening I'd got the little'uns settled and was about to go to bed myself when I heard the back door rattling. Daddy was out, as usual, and Mammy was shut inside her bedroom. I looked out of the window and saw my cousin Mary waving up at me.

'Let me in,' she said. 'Quickly. I've got something dead important to tell you.'

I switched on the landing light then walked downstairs into the kitchen, unlocked the door and saw Mary standing there, grinning at me a bit weirdly.

'What's wrong?' I said.

'Me and Shane are running away,' she said.

'You fuckin' eedjit,' I replied immediately. 'Are ya mad? Are ya a total eedjit?'

'I love him,' she said, clearly a bit put out that I wasn't more enthusiastic.

'Your Daddy's going to go mental,' I went on. 'And it's not the right thing to do. What about the shame of it?'

'It'll be fine,' she said. 'Why don't you and Stevie come with us?'

'Come with yous?' I said. 'No way am I coming with yous. You must think I'm as stupid as you are.'

It was then I noticed another couple of shapes in the shadows on the back step – it was Mary's boyfriend Shane

and with him was Stevie. He stepped up to the door and
grabbed my hand. He was red-faced and I could tell by the
way he was lurching around that he'd been drinking. 'If
you loved me you'd come with us,' he said.

'Ah, my Daddy would kill me, Stevie,' I said. 'And you,
come to think of it.'

Me and Stevie had been together a couple of months by
then and although we'd said that we loved each other, it was
still in a pretty childish way. I'd never thought my future
would be with him. But then, to be honest, I don't think I'd
thought about my future full stop.

'Oh but come with us,' he went on. 'We'll go away then
get married and we can go to America.'

'But what about the little'uns? What about Little Danny?'
I said. 'Who'd look after all of them with me gone?'

'We could come back for them,' he laughed. 'And we'll
take them with us . . . to Disney World. We'll all go to
Disney World. You've always wanted to see it haven't you?'

I was frowning now. I knew this was a ridiculous plan
but I could feel myself beginning to be swept along with it
regardless. On one level it seemed like just another of
Stevie's crazy ideas. What harm could it do really? And
things at home were so desperate. It certainly sounded a
whole lot more exciting than another night stuck in front
of *Corrie* while the kids slept upstairs.

'Please, Rosie,' Mary joined in again.

'If I go on my own with Shane I'll have a bad name for
the rest of my life. But if you come too it won't be so bad.'

I hesitated as the reality of what we were talking about
hit me again. I knew that if we went away with the lads
we'd both have to marry them – that was how it worked in

traveller culture. But at least if we went together our reputations wouldn't be totally destroyed. By going I would be making things better for Mary. If she went alone she risked being disowned by her family and drummed out of the traveller community. Mary was headstrong though. Once she'd made up her mind to do something, nothing would stop her.

But I wasn't desperate to marry Stevie at all. Then again, I didn't hate him either.

It is hard to explain this whole crazy situation to someone who isn't a traveller but the best I can say is that when virtually everyone you know is married in their teens it's not such a big deal. We're not like country people who have relationship after relationship, live with people, split up with them and take decades to decide who they really want to marry. With us it is a decision we almost all make when we're still kids. I, certainly, was a total child at this point.

'OK,' I said. 'I'll do it.'

I could say that I was madly in love with Stevie or that I agreed because I was scared of him. But neither of those was true. I was simply a total eedjit. I gave it about as much thought as whether I wanted vinegar on my chips. I might have been able to hold down a job and look after a family but when it came to serious stuff like this, I had the brain of a five-year-old.

I knew that once I'd been away with Stevie for a night I'd have to marry him or spend the rest of my life living with such a stigma that no one else would ever marry me.

And once a traveller girl married, that was it, for life. Divorce wasn't an option. But I was too young and daft to have any concept of what 'the rest of my life' actually meant. I could barely think about next week, let alone 40 years' time. And I certainly had no idea what married life would be like. I'd seen Mammy and Daddy together and all my aunties and uncles but I didn't really know what it meant to be attached to someone else until your dying day. How could I? I was totally inexperienced.

I'm sure that part of me was looking for a way to escape everything that had been going on at home. But I don't think I even thought about that very deeply. In fact I'm pretty sure I wasn't thinking at all. I didn't really love Stevie, he didn't really love me, I wasn't pregnant and there was absolutely no reason why we should run away. But we were kids and the whole thing seemed like a bit of a laugh.

'Come on then,' laughed Stevie.

So I went – there and then.

I didn't pack any clothes, not even a toothbrush or any money. I simply pulled the back door closed behind me and ran down the path. It felt just like another of the scrapes I'd got into with Marty and Chrissie – I didn't think how much more serious it was going to be this time.

'Where are we going to anyways?' I asked.

'London,' replied Mary. 'There's a priest there that'll marry us.'

We walked down to the canal and along the towpath.

'We'll go down the other side of town and find a car,' said Stevie.

Me and Shane were the more sensible of the four of us – although not much more! We hung back, giggling, as we watched the other two go striding off ahead.

'Are we dreaming this Shane?' I asked. 'Pinch me will ya? I'm sure I must be asleep.'

Every now and then we touched the wall by the side of the canal just to make sure it was real.

'We're going to get battered for this,' I giggled. But still we carried on.

It felt like we walked for hours until the path veered off into a housing estate on the other side of town to where we lived. Stevie and Shane started trying car door handles to look for one left unlocked that we could nick to take us to London. I'd never been in a stolen car before but I knew the boys hotwired cars if they needed to get somewhere.

After a while we came to an all-night garage and stopped to buy sweets and drinks.

'Well if I'm getting married I'll have a jumbo bottle of pop,' I said, demanding Stevie get me a massive four-litre one. That's how mature I was! Of course I didn't think that I'd then have to lug the bottle for another three miles as we continued to look for a car in which to make our escape.

Finally the boys found a little Volkswagen Polo that some poor owner had left unlocked by the side of their house. Stevie fiddled around for a while under the steering column until the engine burst into life.

'Get in yous lot,' he yelled and we all jumped in, leaving the doors open until we reached the end of the road in case we woke up the owner by slamming them shut.

'Oh Jesus, we're going to go to jail,' I wailed in the back. I pulled my cardigan sleeves down over my hands and wouldn't touch anything in case I left fingerprints. But the boys didn't give a shit. They were drunk and were yelling and laughing as they drove along. Looking back it was so dangerous and so stupid and wrong, but like I say, back then I was a total eedjit.

We followed the road signs out of town onto the motorway and south to London. This really was an adventure. I'd been to London travelling to see cousins once or twice before but that had been years earlier and always with Mammy and Daddy.

This time felt very different indeed.

It was light by the time we arrived at Shane's aunt's house in east London. When we banged on the door we had to wait for ages before she answered it, wearing a lilac satin kimono-type dressing gown. She looked dead exotic although she spoke with a strong cockney accent.

'Can we come in Auntie Anne?' said Shane. 'We've run away from home and we're going to get married as soon as we can find somewhere to do it.'

Auntie Anne stared at us in horror. 'What've you done?' she said. 'You're children, just children. What are your daddies goin' to say about this? Get outta here and get yourselves straight to that phone box on the end of the road and tell your families where y'are.'

Tommy and Shane were both so worried about what us girls' daddies would say that when we got to the phone box they decided to pretend to be each other. I'm not sure how that helped but it meant Shane rang my daddy and Stevie rang Mary's. My daddy went pure mental mad when Shane introduced himself as Stevie and said we'd run away together to London.

'You get your fecking arse back here right now,' Daddy yelled down the phone. 'I'm going to fecking kill you – and that daughter o'mine.'

Shane was so terrified he slammed the receiver down and we ran off down the road. Now knowing how mad our parents were about us running away, we felt more compelled than ever to go through with our double wedding.

Stevie had a cousin who lived nearby and she pointed us in the direction of a priest who was known to marry traveller kids who had run away from home. It was a fairly common occurrence. We went to his church and banged on the door.

'Please, Father, will you marry us?' asked Stevie, when the old priest finally tottered out to see us.

He looked at each one of us for an age, nodding slowly. 'How old are you then, dear?' he said, staring at me.

I paused for a bit.

'When's your birthday, girl?' he repeated, obviously thinking I was a bit backward.

'Er, well, I don't really know,' I said slowly. It sounds incredible but I actually had no idea. I thought I was 17 but I didn't know for certain and I hadn't the faintest clue when my birthday was – we'd never celebrated them since I'd been a toddler.

The priest turned to Mary and repeated his questions. She stared at him equally blankly.

Neither of us knew how old we were but we clearly looked far too young to marry without parental permission.

'Go home to your families and get yourselves to school,' the priest said and quietly closed the door.

We stood around the outside of the church, none of us quite sure what to do next.

There was only really one option.

'Best go back then,' said Mary, who already had tears running down her face, considering the beating she'd be getting from her daddy.

It felt like the drive back up the M6 took about five days as we each sat quietly thinking about what awaited us when we got there. Us girls now had the shame of having been away overnight with a boy, but without even having got married.

I'd run away without even a door key so when I got home to our house I had to press Mammy's three-chime doorbell and wait on the step in terror for it to be opened.

Daddy flung open the door and pushed straight past me looking for Stevie but he was already long gone. He wasn't going to be hanging around to see my daddy just then.

Daddy then grabbed me by the back of my cardi and hauled me into the front room where he went clean mental. 'People'll call you a whore,' he kept saying. 'Don't you understand? Don't you care?'

'I'm sorry, Daddy,' I said, crying and crying. 'I didn't think.'

It felt like an age but finally he let me out of the room and I trudged upstairs to my bedroom. Bridget and the little'uns were already there, lined up on the bed waiting for me.

'Where've you been?' asked Tina.

'Are you really married?' giggled Maria.

'Mammy's gone,' said Bridget.

'What?' I said.

'She's gone. Walked out and left him. Daddy was so angry when he got the phone call from yous in London that he went clean mad at Mammy saying she was a disgrace and it was all her fault 'cos she hadn't been there to advise us girls proper. Then he swung round and slapped her. Mammy said she'd had enough what with him and the whore an' all and she was off. We haven't seen her since.'

Bridget and I spent that evening ringing round family trying to find out if anyone had seen or heard from Mammy. Nothing. She had totally disappeared.

The next morning our chiming doorbell gave out its 'dong ding dong' again. It was Stevie. He barely looked at me as he came down the hall and sat down with Daddy in the front room. We all knew why he was there. He hadn't discussed it with me but it was what had to be done in the traveller world. I guess his parents had told him there was no choice.

'Excuse me, Mr McKinley,' he said, all polite and humble. 'May I ask for your daughter's hand in marriage?'

Daddy growled at him, 'OK.' Then he went back to glaring at the TV.

Daddy didn't really want me to marry Stevie; he'd warned me off him from the beginning. But now I'd run away with him, Daddy had no choice but to let us marry. I was spoiled goods. It was totally crazy really considering I was still a virgin.

So that was it. My fate was pretty much sealed. And in the cold light of day I was beginning to wonder about whether the whole marriage thing was actually a very bad idea. Stevie was a laugh alright, but deep down I knew that crazy side that I'd been so attracted to at first would mean nothing but trouble in the long term. I tried to put those doubts out of my mind. Like an eedjit I just went with the flow.

It was another three days before Mammy rolled home. She was stinking, filthy and in a terrible state from drink. It looked like nothing was getting any better at home and I thought marriage might at least be an escape from it all.

Me and Stevie went to the priest and booked a date for the wedding in eight months' time. Stevie announced he wanted to earn some more money for us to set up home. One of his cousins in Cornwall had work going so he set off down there.

Daddy couldn't give a damn about the wedding and Mammy was barely sober long enough to discuss it.

When Bridget had got married it'd been a nice do with family coming from all over the country for a hot, sit-down reception in the church hall. But with my wedding no one even seemed to give a thought to any of the preparations. I was due to wear Bridget's old wedding dress, which was way too big for me as I was still a boyish, size eight figure. But no one else seemed bothered that I'd be in a frock three sizes too big, so I didn't let it bother me either.

At first Stevie came back from Cornwall every weekend to see me but as the months slipped by he returned less and less. Then the phone calls stopped coming so frequently too. 'I didn't have any coins for the phone box,' he'd say when he finally called after a fortnight's silence.

'Oh aye,' I'd say. I wasn't distraught when I didn't hear from him for weeks on end because rather than absence making the heart grow fonder, it had actually just made me realise my feelings maybe weren't as strong as they ought to have been. I knew that despite the fun and excitement we'd had together, I wasn't really in love with him. We were just two kids on a wedding conveyor belt because our parents had told us it was the right thing to do.

Then Daddy got word from someone in the traveller community that Stevie had been going steady with another girl down in Cornwall. Daddy was furious. 'That fecking little shit,' he seethed, bursting in from the pub to tell me one night. 'I'll beat him black and blue when I see him,' he said, obviously forgetting about his own dubious behaviour.

'Oh,' I said when Daddy told me the news. I didn't ring Stevie or confront him about it. I wasn't quite sure what to do. 'I'll deal with this,' Daddy said. And I knew that he would. Quietly though I think both Daddy and I were partly relieved at the news. It gave me the perfect opportunity to break off the engagement. There was going to be no wedding.

Daddy made sure the news filtered back to Stevie through his family that the marriage was off.

I knew my reputation would take a bit of a slagging because I wasn't marrying the man I'd run away with, but he had cheated on me, so maybe there would be some sympathy with me because of that. It was hard for a long time though. If I went to a travellers' disco or out for a few drinks with mates you'd think I had some kind of contagious disease. Blokes wouldn't even come near me because I'd run away with a man and been engaged to him but not married. I was damaged goods in their eyes and didn't I know it. It felt as though everywhere I went, people were whispering about me. I thought I was going to be stuck on the shelf for the rest of my life.

One evening I went to a travellers' disco with my aunt Chrissie and uncle Marty. Me and Chrissie were standing chatting while Marty queued at the bar to get us a couple of Martini and Lemonades (we thought that was dead classy!). A lad we knew from one of the sites came over and started asking Chrissie if she'd been to the Pizza Hut that had just opened in the town.

'Apparently the pizzas are massive,' I giggled, trying to join in the conversation.

'Well I wouldna worry yourself about that,' he shot back, barely turning his face to me. 'No fella will be taking you for a pizza there or anywhere else.'

I didn't say a word. Neither did Chrissie. I guess we both knew he was right. Even boys I hadn't even met knew enough about me now to make sure they weren't seen dead with me.

Sometimes I'd lie in bed at night and wonder what would become of me. I'd been brought up being taught that the only thing a woman should do was get married and have kids. And now it looked like no man would ever want me. What else was there left for me? I had absolutely no idea. I tried not to think about it. Maybe Stevie would come back one day. Maybe he wouldn't.

I didn't hear a word from Stevie for nine months – not a single phone call or message. I went back to concentrating on my job and looking after the kids at home. I was learning the hard way what it meant to have a bad reputation in the travelling community.

11

Marriage

Then one day Stevie turned up again. I'd just got back from Morrisons in the town and was unpacking the shopping when the doorbell rung. When I opened it I was still holding a packet of pork pies in my hand.

'These for me?' that familiar voice said, grabbing the pies out of my hand and ripping open the packet. 'My favourite.'

'What are ya doin'?' I choked.

'Just remembering what I've been missing,' he replied, staring up at me with that cheeky gaze. 'And I don't just mean the pies,' he said.

'You'd better come in,' I replied. And as I walked back to the kitchen with him munching on that bloody pie behind me, scattering crumbs all down the carpet, I knew I was lost. However hurt I'd been, however angry, I still wanted to be with him. Maybe it wasn't love like a lot of people know it, but it was something near enough. Stevie was fun and he seemed to like me. And he was an escape from the drudgery and hard slog of my life. And after months of thinking no man would ever look at me again, it was nice to know Stevie was still interested.

'I want us to get back together,' Stevie said as I boiled the kettle.

'OK,' I replied. I'd like to say I played it cool or gave him a terrible ear-bashing for the way he'd treated me. But the truth is I didn't. I was grateful he was there. Grateful that someone, anyone, was paying an interest in me. So there was no drama, no rows and no tears. It might sound crazy but I never asked about the other woman or what he'd been up to. I guess I just didn't want to know. It was enough that he still liked me and getting married would finally shake off the bad name I'd been stuck with since we first ran away together. It might sound like I was a pinball being fired around in different directions with no control over my life. And yes, my life was kind of like that for a long time. I knew though that once we were married I'd be considered respectable again – I could worry about what it meant to be a wife afterwards.

I knew Daddy would be furious if he thought I was going back with Stevie, so I simply didn't tell him.

'Let's run away again,' Stevie said. 'But this time we'll get married properly and we'll come back as man and wife.'

Stevie knew of a priest up in Glasgow who would marry travellers there and then on the spot without asking too many questions about their background. It sounded grand.

I rang Bridget who was still living just at the bottom of the road and told her what I was going to do. She helped me mind the little'uns most days when I was at work so she'd be able to look out for them while I was gone.

'Are you sure this is a good idea?' said Bridget.

'Not really,' I replied. 'But I'm gonna do it anyways. I don't want to spend the rest of my life in this house listening to Mammy and Daddy rowing every night. And there's no other way out for me. Hopefully I'll soon be able to come back for the little'uns. It'll be better for everyone.

'OK. Well ring me when you get there,' she said.

I left Bridget to tell Mammy and Daddy where I'd gone. And I asked her to call my work and say I wouldn't be coming back. I felt awful letting them down like that but once I was married there was no question I'd be able to work anyway. I'd never met a married traveller woman with a job. It just never happened.

'Tell them I'm sorry, B,' I said. And I was sorry, so sorry. I'd loved that job so much. I think that was maybe why I couldn't bring myself to ring them to tell them I wouldn't be going back. I couldn't quite believe it myself.

So me and Stevie set off in his Ford Escort, racing up the motorway so fast that I felt sick.

When we got to the priest's house, his housekeeper answered the door.

'Is the Father in?' Stevie asked, all polite. 'We want him to marry us today.'

The housekeeper smiled. 'Oh, I'm sorry,' she said. 'He retired yesterday – he's gone off on a well-deserved holiday.'

I felt even sicker. It looked like I was never going to get married.

The housekeeper pointed us in the direction of another Catholic priest in the city. He was lovely to us and said he'd be delighted to marry us – but in three months' time! There was no way he was going to break the rules and we'd have to wait for the banns to be read all proper. But there was no way I could wait that long. If I stayed away from home with Stevie for three months my reputation would be destroyed forever.

'We'll have to go to London again,' Stevie said. 'I'm sorry, Rosie, but it'll have to be a register office wedding. I've got a cousin down there, she can be our witness.'

So we set off southwards. We'd been driving for almost 24 hours when we finally found a register office in north London that would marry us the following day.

We went to stay at Stevie's cousin's house and she managed to borrow a white dress for me from a friend. There were wine stains down the front of the frock and it gaped around the armpits but at least it was white. Well, whiteish, anyway. I nipped out to the shops and bought some starch for the veil and then we went to a jeweller's to choose matching wedding rings and bought a bunch of flowers for me to hold.

I was up virtually all night scrubbing that dress, starching it and then drying it with a hairdryer. Stevie's cousin was lovely and very kind but we were all struggling to get excited about the day.

I felt sick with nerves. What if I got my vows wrong? Or if I tripped on the dress? There were so many things that could go wrong. And underneath all these worries there was a terrible feeling of heartbreak. I was so sad that my brothers and sisters weren't there to see me and I was sad too that my parents weren't there. But I knew I was thinking about Mammy and Daddy as they had been in the past, before Mammy started drinking and Daddy started carrying-on.

I told myself that maybe when I was married and my bad reputation was forgotten by other travellers then things might go back to normal. At least my shame would be gone. It still didn't really enter my brain though that this was the rest of my life that I was committing myself to. I was like a child doing something I really didn't understand.

The next morning I got up and put on my dress and veil.

There was a full-length mirror on the inside of the wardrobe and even I could see I looked a right state. The veil stuck out at an odd angle where it hadn't starched properly and there was still a smudge of red wine down the front of the dress. It hung baggily around my chest and was a good two inches too long at the bottom. My hair was crinkly from where I'd put in Stevie's cousin's rollers the night before. I looked like a clown. Years before Mammy would have died to see her daughter turned out like this on her wedding day. Now she didn't even know I was getting wed. Just thinking about that made me a bit tearful.

Two of Stevie's sisters turned up and tried to help me fix the dress at the back.

I looked at them and started crying. 'It's not fair,' I choked. 'Stevie has got you two and all his cousins here and I've got no one.' I felt utterly alone. But the worst thing was I knew I'd brought it all upon myself.

The service was over in a matter of minutes and then we filed out with Stevie's family and straight into a pub across the road.

There was a big group of friends and cousins sitting around a table, drinking pint after pint of strong lager. Then they started rolling cannabis joints with Rizla papers. I wasn't into any of that at all. Daddy had always warned us to keep well clear of drugs and I knew he'd be horrified that this was going on just a couple of hours after my wedding.

'Stevie, that man over there is making drugs,' I said, pulling Stevie's sleeve.

But my new husband just turned round to me and laughed. 'Yeah?' he said. 'And in a minute I'm going to be smoking them!'

I knew Stevie was no angel and he certainly liked a drink but I didn't think he'd ever touch drugs. I was totally mad that he'd be smoking dope at our wedding reception.

'Are ya now?' I said. 'Well in that case I'll be wanting a divorce.'

Stevie just laughed right at me again then went over to his friends and started smoking the joint, blowing the smoke towards me.

'Well fuck you,' I shouted and stormed out of the pub. I was raging and stomped down the street in my massive wedding dress yelling, 'I want a divorce.'

A bus driver hooted his horn at me and people walking in the other direction were either laughing or looking at me as if I were totally mad.

After half an hour I was just about calm enough to go back to the pub. Stevie was still drinking heavily and smoking the joints with his mates.

'Just chill out, Rosie,' Stevie said when he saw me. 'You can't get addicted to it.'

'I don't care whether you can or you can't,' I said. 'You can stick your drugs where the sun don't shine.'

'Just because we're married doesn't mean you're going to be able to control me, y'know,' he said.

'We'll see about that,' I snapped. But I think in honesty I already knew he was right and I had little chance of controlling my wayward new husband.

By the end of the night Stevie was so wasted he fell into bed unconscious. I was in no rush to lose my virginity, I'd heard about how horrific that could be, but it was still a dismal end to a crap day – my wedding day.

The next morning we set off back home to tell Mammy

and Daddy that we were married. Stevie was hungover and grumpy. I was still in a foul temper and terrified about how Daddy was going to react. We also had other news – Stevie had booked us both to fly out to Germany the next morning. He had a lot of family members who travelled around Germany in the Black Forest areas and they had promised him work. 'It'll be a new start to married life,' he said.

'OK,' I replied. It did sound exciting.

When we got home to Manchester it was around teatime.

'We're married, Daddy,' I said, as he opened the front door to the pair of us.

'You'd best come in then,' he replied. I could tell Daddy was angry but he was keeping a lid on it. 'I'm not happy,' he said to Stevie as we sat in the front room. 'But I s'pose you're married now so at least you won't be able to bring any more shame on this family.'

That night I slept with little Danny again as I had done almost every night since he'd been born. I still had no desire to sleep with my husband and I couldn't bear to waste a moment away from the little boy I'd brought up pretty much as my own. I'd hated being away from him for just two nights so the thought of going away again for months – maybe even years – made me feel sick. Danny was almost four by then but he still needed regular treatment for his delayed and physiotherapy development.

'I'll be back in a couple of months,' I told Danny that night. 'And Bridget will be here to look after you anyway. And I'll call every single week, I promise.'

I couldn't stop sobbing as I packed my case the following morning. Suddenly the thought of leaving my family to be with a husband I barely knew and his family seemed a lot less appealing than it had when I was so desperate to escape from the poisonous atmosphere at home.

'You've made your bed, Rosie,' Daddy said. 'Now you'll have to lie in it.' Those words were to haunt me for years afterwards.

We set off that morning for Germany. Stevie's brother, Joey, came with us and for the first week or so we travelled together from motel to motel.

'You can bunk down with us,' I said to Joey that first night and from then he did it every night. It was the perfect way to keep Stevie off me.

I was terrified about losing my virginity. 'It's worse than getting murdered,' my auntie Chrissie had told me years before, as we swapped what little information about sex we did possess. 'My mammy says she would rather have ten children than sleep with my daddy,' said another cousin. Gruesome tales of women soaking the bed in blood and screaming out in pain had totally put me off the whole idea.

But as day after day passed, Stevie became increasingly unhappy that his wife wasn't showing any interest in him sexually. 'You're frigid,' he said one night, trying to get his hands under my top as I pushed them away.

'I don't care what I am,' I said. 'You're not touching me!'

I'd spent so many years thinking that it was utterly wrong for a man to touch my skin, let alone anything else, that it was hard to get my head around the idea that now a fella was allowed to do whatever he wanted to me. To me, it didn't really make any difference that he was my husband.

Despite my terror of sex, me and Stevie were getting on

quite well. And slowly I really could feel as though I were falling in love with him. There was no doubt he was what Daddy would call a 'bad lad'. He liked drinking and smoking and fighting and had little interest in working. Yet despite that he could make me laugh like no one else had ever done.

Back home my life had been all about cooking, cleaning, looking after the little'us, running around after Daddy and caring for Mammy. My new life was just about me and Stevie and having a laugh together. I liked it.

We'd been married a fortnight when I finally ran out of good reasons as to why Stevie and I shouldn't sleep together. By then his cousin Joey had been joined by his wife so he was no longer bunking on our floor and they'd moved into their own motel room.

One evening I knew that it was going to be 'the night' so I made sure our bedroom was as far from Joey's as possible. If losing my virginity was like being murdered I didn't want all Stevie's family hearing about it! To get to our room in the motel you turned right out of the reception area and walked and walked for ages. To get to Joey and his wife's room you turned left out of reception and carried on walking.

But what I didn't realise was that the hotel was actually a circular design.

That night I finally let Stevie have his way. It wasn't that bad, although Stevie made quite a lot of noise, which I found a bit alarming. But it was certainly nothing like the Hammer Horror stories that my cousins had peddled. In fact, it was getting light by the time we finally went to sleep.

Next morning at breakfast, Joey's wife looked knack-ered. Joey was in a foul mood. 'There was a couple in the room next to us at it all night,' Joey said. 'It was a disgrace. I tried knocking on the door but they couldn't even hear me.'

I looked down at the hotel door key lying next to his cereal bowl. It was number 1578. I carefully slid my hand over the door key lying on my lap – number 1579! Our rooms must actually have been next to each other.

A couple of days later we arrived at the trailer site in Germany and were met by dozens of Stevie's relatives. Each day Stevie and his brothers would go out doing building work on a massive new housing development nearby which was being staffed almost entirely by English travellers. I'd stay at the trailer, chatting with the other women, tidying up and preparing dinner. Sometimes we'd go out shopping or for a coffee in the nearest town.

I picked up a couple of German words but most of the places we went everyone spoke English.

When we were together, me and Stevie got on well. We shared the same childish sense of humour and were more like mates than husband and wife. They were good times and I think by then I was in love with my new husband. But I quickly became aware that if there was drinking and partying to be done, I would always come a poor third to those.

Stevie started going out most evenings with his cousins and friends on the site. There are thousands of British trav-ellers in Germany and most of them seem to know each other or are related in some way.

After years of living in our council house in Manchester,

I liked being back in the trailer again. I was able to play 'house' with my own trailer, making it all nice and keeping it clean and tidy the way Mammy had done when we were kids. Sometimes I thought back to the job I'd had as a chef or how I'd thought about being independent and supporting myself. But here I was being a typical traveller wife to a typical traveller husband. Most of the time it didn't bother me. Yes, Stevie would go out with his mates on drinking sessions, roll home in the early hours then expect me to sleep with him. But I didn't complain – it was what us women expected.

I missed home badly though, particularly little Danny. I rang home at least once a week but the reception was often bad. All my brothers and sisters would come on the phone one by one and it'd break my heart to think of them crowded around the receiver at the bottom of the hall. As the months went by I hated the idea that they were growing up without me around. Mammy was no better but I knew Bridget was looking after them all well. It didn't stop me missing them though.

We'd been in Germany about seven months when I missed my yokes. I knew enough then to know that meant I was pregnant. All the other women on the site had been asking me almost daily if I was in the 'family way' yet. Seven months with no sign of a pregnancy was considered unusual among traveller women. So when I did realise I'd fallen, it almost came as a relief – I was just like the other women after all.

My yokes was about ten days late when I broke the news to Stevie. He'd been working all day and was having a wash at the kitchen sink and I could tell he was in a rush to meet his mates down the bar. But I couldn't wait a minute longer.

'So, Stevie,' I said. 'How would ya feel about being a daddy then?'

He spun round, soap suds still all over his face.

'What?' he said. 'Are ya? Are ya?' It was like he didn't want to use the actual word. Traveller men didn't talk about that sort of thing.

'Yep,' I giggled. 'We're going to have a baby. We're going to be a mammy and a daddy.'

Stevie leaned towards me and kissed me that rough way he had when he first grabbed me. I knew things weren't perfect between us but I desperately hoped this baby would solve our problems. And he was still a great kisser.

Stevie's parents were back in England then and we both decided we wanted to be back home, near our parents for the birth. So we set off back westwards.

I'd travelled around all my life but there was only ever one home – with my family. I was delighted to be going back.

12

New Baby, Missing Husband ·

I didn't even need to step in our front door to see that home was getting less and less like the place I remembered. There were thick weeds out the front and the curtains were falling down at the windows. Mammy had become so sick with the drink that the kids were spending most of their time round at Bridget's place. Kevin had gone off to stay with some of our cousins near Leeds.

Daddy was barely ever there. He'd be at home first thing in the morning, still keeping up the pretence that he slept there every night, but we all knew by then it was a lie and that he spent his nights elsewhere.

Mammy was for the most part living alone in total squalor. How could these carpets now thick with grime be the ones she'd Shake and Vac'd to within an inch of their lives? And how could the Crown Derby lined along the kitchen shelf, now grey with fag smoke and dirt, be the same delicate dinner service that she had once washed and polished every single day?

But even more shocking than all of that was the state of Mammy herself. She was now unrecognisable as the 80s power-dressing vamp that I'd idolised. She looked like a down and out, a street drinker – which is exactly what she had become. She was now regularly going missing for days on end and as soon as I returned to Manchester I was back to the trips out with Bridget, searching the streets for Mammy in case this time she really had drunk herself to death. We would walk up and down, going in shops and pubs, looking on park benches and talking to tramps until we found her and guided her home.

One night, after dragging her home, I helped her into bed, peeled off her trousers and sat on the bed next to her, feeling utterly exhausted. My head was in my hands and I'd given up trying to fight the tears.

'Mammy, this has got to stop,' I said. 'You're killing yourself and I don't know what to do anymore.'

Mammy reached out and squeezed my hand, but she couldn't even lift her head from the pillow.

'Please, Mammy,' I went on. 'I'm begging you. Please, you must stop drinking.'

For ages there was no sound other than the noise of Mammy's rasping breathing.

'I'm sorry,' she said finally, so quietly I could only just hear her.

But I knew what she was saying. It wasn't so much that she was sorry all of this had happened. She was just sorry she couldn't stop it. This was never going to end, I knew that then.

I kissed her forehead, pulled a blanket up to her chin and walked out of the room.

Me and Stevie moved into a trailer near Mammy and Bridget's houses but I spent most of my time at one or the other place helping out.

I was getting bigger and bigger by the day as the baby's due date got closer. Mammy had no interest in the baby – or anything other than vodka. But Daddy was excited about becoming a grandad again. Bridget had by then had two little boys, TJ (Tommy Jnr) who was three and ten-month-old Davey.

Me and Daddy hadn't really spoken to each other after my wedding until I told him I was pregnant. Then his whole attitude softened and within a few weeks of my return from Germany he was constantly turning up at our trailer with bags of toys and baby clothes. He even bought me a brand-new buggy and a beautiful oak cot that was fit for a prince or princess!

But sadly Stevie didn't share his excitement. In fact the further the pregnancy progressed, the less interest he showed in either me or the baby. Back in Manchester he was far more interested in going out with his mates than being with me. He was doing a bit of labouring when the work came up but mostly he wanted to party. Regularly he would go out on a Friday night and not come back till Sunday teatime.

'Where the hell have you been?' I'd scream when he finally reappeared.

'Just leave it Rosie,' he'd say. 'Leave it, leave it, leave it.'

That was all I ever heard from him. But it was clear that was exactly what he wanted, to be left alone to do what he liked, whenever he liked. And like an eedjit most of the time I did let him get on with it. We were still just children and I don't think either of us realised the seriousness of being married, let alone becoming parents. If he wanted to go off with his mates, I didn't really know how to stop him.

As the time for the birth got closer though, I got more frustrated by Stevie's constant drinking and partying. I was feeling fat and unattractive and the last thing I wanted was a boozed-up bloke rolling in before dawn breathing beer fumes all over me.

My feet were swollen and my back ached but still I was up before seven every morning, making breakfast and cleaning up the trailer while he was lying in bed, sleeping off his hangover.

I'd been surrounded by women all my life who popped out kids like it was nothing more complicated than going to the dentist. But incredible as this might sound, I'd still never asked or been told, exactly what happened when the baby was born. Travellers don't talk about that sort of thing, it would be shameful. So when the pains started real bad, I tried to hide it from everyone. We were round at Stevie's sister's trailer when I first felt a bad contraction. I gritted my teeth and dug my fingernails into the side of the sofa.

'Rosie, are you getting pains?' his sister asked me.

'No, I am not,' I replied. I was too embarrassed to tell the truth. And certainly I would never have imagined talking about a woman's issue like that in front of a man, even if he was my husband. No, I thought the best thing was grit my teeth and hopefully the pains might go away. But instead they kept coming stronger and stronger every few minutes until it was perfectly obvious to everyone that the baby was on its way.

Finally Stevie got me into his van and drove me to the hospital. He took me to the maternity unit then hung around outside. Traveller men weren't expected to be at births but my sister Bridget came up to be with me.

I still had no idea what was going on and when the nurse

offered me gas and air for the pain, I thought it was for my asthma.

'No, my breathing is OK at the moment,' I said. 'It's just these pains in my belly that are the problem.'

'I know, dear,' the nurse said patiently. 'This will make them easier to cope with.'

I was so naïve I honestly didn't know exactly how a baby came out. We had been brought up in such a way that such questions weren't even thought about, let alone asked.

Labour dragged on for 12 hours and as it continued, I truly thought I was dying. Bridget had had to go home after a few hours because she had no one to look after her kids so I was totally on my own apart from the midwives who kept coming and going out of the room.

Finally a nurse said to me, 'You can push now.' I didn't know how it would help but did as I was told, raised my arms above my head and pushed back on the bed frame.

'What are you doing?' asked the nurse.

'You told me to push,' I said. I really hadn't got a clue.

'Not like that,' she said. 'You'll know what I mean when the time comes.'

Twenty minutes later the pain was even more extreme and the baby still wasn't coming out.

'Right, I think we are going to have to cut you,' the nurse said, standing over me with a doctor.

But half an hour after that and still the pain was only getting worse.

'You said you were going to cut me,' I yelled. 'Can't you just get on with it and get this baby out?'

'We have already cut you,' the nurse said.

'Where?' I asked, looking down and seeing no marks on my belly where I'd expected to see a big incision.

'Around your vagina, down below of course,' the nurse said.

'What?' I screeched between contractions. 'What did you cut me there for?'

'Because that's where the baby comes out,' she said, obviously a bit confused as to why I was asking.

I'd been in so much pain from the contractions that I hadn't even felt the small cut that the surgeon must have made to get the baby out. At that point, just minutes from giving birth, I still didn't really understand where the baby would emerge from.

Finally our daughter Sarah-Jane was born. It was just before midnight on April 22, 1988. I was 18 years old.

Sarah-Jane had come out covered in greeny coloured goo. 'Eugh, what's that?' I said.

The nurse explained it was the fluid that had been surrounding the baby inside me.

'Maybe you'd prefer it if I cleaned her up before you held her,' she said.

When she reappeared with the baby wrapped in a blanket a couple of minutes later I was instantly besotted. She was gorgeous.

Sarah-Jane was a very healthy 9lb 2oz with chubby red cheeks and fists clenched as if she was about to start a brawl right there in the delivery room. Stevie came in to see her and looked at the baby with pure happiness.

'Would ya like to hold her?' I asked Stevie.

'Er, I don't know,' he said. Traveller men didn't have much to do with babies, it wasn't thought to be manly. 'Maybe just for a wee second,' he said, reaching out to take her.

It was obvious that Stevie was desperate to hold his first child. He laid her into the crook of his arm and wrapped her tiny hand around his big clumpy finger,

'She's beautiful,' he said. 'Just beautiful.'

'Yeah,' I said. 'She is.'

I couldn't stop looking at her, neither of us could. I'd raised my brothers and sisters since they were babies but having a child of my own was a totally different feeling to anything I'd experienced before.

The following day I was released from hospital and Stevie drove me back to the trailer. But I'd barely got Sarah-Jane in the door when Stevie announced he was going out.

'You're what?' I said. 'I've got a brand-new baby here.'

'Oh leave it Rosie, I'm just meeting a few of the lads to wet the baby's head.'

'No you're not,' I said, picking up Sarah-Jane out of her baby basket. 'We need you here. It's our first night home together.'

Stevie snapped. 'Don't you fucking tell me what I can and cannot do,' he snarled.

I didn't see it happen so there was no warning. But I felt it. A sharp smack across the side of my right cheek. I lurched backwards, gripping Sarah-Jane as I stumbled. Stevie had never hit me before and the shock was as bad as the pain.

I'm not sure why he chose then for the first slap, the moment I was holding our baby in our home for the very first time. Maybe he suddenly realised he was no longer centre of attention and he didn't like it. Maybe he just wanted to make it clear that he was still in charge.

My face stung like mad and tears immediately welled up

in my eyes but I tried my hardest to stop them from spilling down my cheeks.

'You bastard,' I choked back. 'Think you're a big man hitting a woman with a wee baby?'

Slap. There he went again with another smack down the other side of my face. Then he picked up his jacket and walked out.

I'd never felt so lonely and I really didn't know what to do. Mammy was no good to anyone by then and in my head I kept hearing what Daddy had said the day after we married: 'You've made your bed, now you must lie in it.' He was right. I knew the traveller code. I was a wife for life no matter what my husband did. So there was no point in complaining, I just had to get on with it. So I fed the baby, put her into the new pink sleepsuit Bridget had bought, and laid her down in the cot next to our bed. The bed that I'd made, as Daddy would have said . . .

The next morning, Daddy and our Bridget came round to see the baby.

'She's beautiful,' Bridget said, transfixed by the child. But I knew Daddy wasn't looking at his granddaughter – his eyes were focused on the side of my face. There was a red mark down one side and a cut on my cheekbone where Stevie's ring had caught it.

'What's happened to you?' said Daddy.

'Oh, nothing,' I laughed. 'Nothing at all Daddy, I'm grand, I just knocked myself when I got up in the night to feed the baby.'

At that moment I was desperate to tell him the truth so he would put his arms round me and tell me everything would be OK. But I was too scared, frightened of the almighty great fight that would follow and scared too that Daddy might be cross with me again for marrying Stevie in the first place.

So I said nothing and just carried on smiling.

Stevie came back the following afternoon and continued as though nothing had happened. He picked Sarah-Jane up and made baby noises to her as though he was the best daddy in the world.

I've heard stories about men who hit their wives and how the following day they plead for forgiveness and promise it would never happen again, but Stevie never did that. He simply walked in and carried on perfectly normal. There were no apologies, excuses or promises. He just pretended it had never happened. And me, like a jackass, let him. I'd had virtually no sleep and was feeling weepy and exhausted. I didn't have the energy for another fight so I said nothing. I carried on just the same too and prayed that the previous night had been a one-off that would never be repeated.

But of course it was repeated. Stevie's celebrations at becoming a daddy went on for about two months. The baby's head wasn't just wet, it was totally saturated! But every time I'd complain that Stevie was going out with his mates for the twenty-eighth night in a row or had got home late again or that he was lying in bed rather than going out looking for work, there'd be another slap.

Stevie would never give the baby her bottle or get up in the night if she was crying. And Sarah-Jane cried a lot. I'd walk up and down the trailer rocking her until she was just dozing off, then the moment I laid her down in her cot she was wide awake again, screaming the place down. I was at my wits' end. I was surviving on hardly any sleep and was exhausted but there was no way Stevie was going to help out. In the traveller world, babies were women's work.

At Sarah-Jane's christening, Daddy had a couple of drinks and so did I. Everyone told me that Guinness was good for my iron levels!

'Tell me the truth, Rosie,' Daddy said to me. 'Has Stevie been hitting you?'

Again I was so desperate to tell him the truth and for it all to be out in the open but I just couldn't do it. I was terrified that if I told him, he'd go pure mental and I couldn't let it all kick off at my daughter's christening. And for some reason I still felt I had to protect Stevie too. I couldn't admit what had happened.

'No, Daddy,' I said. 'It's just lack of sleep with a new baby, it's making me clumsy.'

I'm sure he didn't believe me but he didn't ask me any more about it.

'Well if anything ever does happen, you be sure to tell me,' he said.

As the weeks went by, Stevie's disappearances became for longer and longer periods. Some of Stevie's family helped me out with Sarah-Jane – they understood things weren't easy and they were good to me. Stevie's mammy had had 21 children and there was nothing she didn't know about looking after a baby. Gradually Sarah-Jane started sleeping more and crying less and things became easier. But still Stevie was rarely around.

One day he went to the pub with his mates and disappeared for more than a week. I couldn't be certain that Stevie was seeing other women but after Daddy's affair I was under no illusions about men any more. I didn't want to believe he was cheating on me and I could never prove anything, but the way he dressed up for a night out, the unexplained absences, the shifty behaviour all made me suspicious. I might have been a pushover but I wasn't totally stupid. But as Stevie didn't carry a mobile phone I never had any way of contacting him when he was out.

Then after one really bad row, he walked out and stayed away for weeks. At first I thought he had gone for good. I knew he wasn't sick or anything because I heard through cousins and friends that he was fit and well and living in London. 'He's down there searching for a bit of work,' one of our cousins told me.

'Oh he is, is he?' I replied. I knew full well the only thing Stevie would be doing in London was downing pints of Guinness and chasing skirt. 'Well you can tell him that when he gets bored and decides to come back again, he's not welcome.'

I didn't really mean it. What I really wanted was for Stevie to come home and be with me and his baby, to be one of those fellas who came straight back from work then sat on the sofa with me watching telly till bedtime. OK, it might not sound exciting to a lot of people, but at least I'd know where he was. I had to face facts though, Stevie wasn't that kind of man. At night when I put Sarah-Jane in her cot and sat on the sofa, that's when I would cry. But I wasn't crying because I'd been abandoned, I was crying because deep down I knew I'd married the wrong man from the start.

At least his absence meant some peace from his unpredictable behaviour but it still hurt that he'd gone off and left me. And I was ashamed too. Daddy had been right about my husband all along. I never thought this was the end of my marriage though. I knew he would be back. That wasn't how it worked for traveller women. I'd still be Stevie's wife, I'd always be Stevie's wife. I just had to learn to put up with him doing whatever it was that he wanted. I had never known anyone who had done any different and divorced their husband. It was totally unheard of. I literally could not imagine anything other than the life I had.

13

Ready to Kill

Weeks drifted into months and still there was no sign of Stevie. Sarah-Jane had learnt to sit up, then crawl, then take her first staggering footsteps across our trailer but her father had missed all these milestones. There seemed little prospect he'd be back any time soon and as I was spending most of my time helping to look after Mammy and my younger brother and sisters, I decided to move back in with them. The little'uns had been staying with Bridget but she had her own family to worry about too.

I spent weeks tarting up Mammy's house, making it fit to live in again. I painted every single room, got new carpets laid and hung clean curtains.

Mammy stayed in her bedroom most of the time and I tried to hide the worst of her drinking from the kids. She would still go out for hours on end though and I'd know that she had been out boozing with some of her drinking pals. Well, they weren't really mates. The only thing they had in common was booze.

One night when Mammy had been gone all day, me and Bridget put our coats on and set out looking for her again. We walked for hours but couldn't find her anywhere and went back to Bridget's. I couldn't sleep for worry and went out looking again during the night, convinced that something real bad had happened this time. I'd only just got back to Bridget's at about half six in the morning when a police car turned up outside. Mammy was in the back seat motionless. Her skin was a blue colour, her lips were purple.

'Jesus, she's dead,' I said.

I shook her but there was no reaction. She was either unconscious or she really was dead. The policeman explained he'd found her lying on a pavement. He'd brought her back countless times before so he knew exactly where we lived. He had seen her in this state so many times before, he hadn't even bothered calling an ambulance.

We carried Mammy into the house and I called our doctor. 'Check her pulse,' she said.

At first there was nothing but gradually I found the faintest movement.

Next I rang an ambulance and paramedics came and gave her an injection, which I think must have been adrenalin to get her heart going again. She was freezing cold and the paramedics wrapped thick blankets all around her.

Suddenly she sat bolt upright. 'I don't want to go to hospital,' she said.

The paramedics were looking very worried. 'You've got to persuade her,' one of them whispered to me. 'She has extremely serious hyperthermia as well as all the damage she has done through alcohol. We can't force her to go but if she doesn't get the treatment she needs pretty quickly she *will* die.'

Me and Bridget were screaming at Mammy who was flitting in and out of consciousness. Finally she nodded and that was enough of an agreement for us. We helped the paramedics lift her into the back of the ambulance and followed them down to the hospital.

At the hospital two doctors spent ages examining her and then came out, looking terrifyingly serious.

Mammy was drifting in and out of consciousness, her blood was coming out of her in clots because of the amount of alcohol in her system and they'd had to drain fluid from her lungs. God only knows what damage she'd done to her liver.

'Your mother really is very sick,' the young doctor told us. 'The next 24 hours are going to be critical to see if she will pull through or not.'

That night me, Bridget, Ol'Mammy, Sean, Tommy, Tina and Auntie Patsy all sat around her bed, willing Mammy to pull through. And, there was Daddy too. No matter what they'd been through together, he still loved her. Daddy leant across and held Mammy's hand. I'd never seen him look so pale and old before. He seemed to have aged 20 years. Maybe it was the guilt. But in a way that just made me madder. If he loved her why had he been carrying on with that young girl for all this time?

'Oh please Jesus, don't let her die,' I prayed over and over again, throughout the night. In many ways our Mammy had left us years earlier – but while she was alive there was always the hope that she might go back to being the woman we'd known when we were kids.

The following morning the doctor came into the waiting room, which by then was packed to the rafters with traveller friends and family. In our culture everyone turns out to show their support if someone is sick.

'Well,' the doctor said looking around the room, not

quite sure who to make eye contact with. 'She seems much better. Hopefully she will pull through but the damage she has done to her liver is still very serious.'

For a couple of days, Mammy made steady progress. Then one morning when I went in to visit her, the doctor called me over. He was furious. 'Someone has been giving your mother alcohol,' he said.

'What?' I replied. Surely she couldn't be drinking again. No. Not after everything she'd been through.

'Last night one of the nurses had her suspicions so she searched her bedside cabinet and found a bottle of vodka and packets of cigarettes,' he fumed. 'Surely it must be clear to anyone that the last thing she needs is to smoke when she is on oxygen because she can barely breathe.'

'This can't go on,' he said, calming down a bit. 'You've got to tell your family that they are killing her.'

I had tears in my eyes but they were tears of anger. I was so mad that some eedjit had thought it OK to give Mammy booze and fags. But I was even more angry that she had taken it. It was at that moment that I realised I was fighting a battle I was never going to win. Mammy was never going to be able to stop drinking. She didn't want to do it.

In our community it would be impossible to stop people from going to visit a relative in hospital – it's just not done. Mammy was already telling her cousins that me and Bridget were treating her like a dog, not letting her do whatever she wanted. And these people were believing her rather than us.

So the hospital arranged for a security guard to be stationed outside Mammy's door with the job of searching everyone's bags before they went in to make sure they weren't smuggling alcohol. Some of our aunties and cousins were outraged at the thought of being searched but we had no choice. It felt like everywhere I turned I was having to fight to keep Mammy alive.

'Is Mammy going to die?' little Danny asked me one night. But he didn't seem upset or scared at the thought, merely curious.

'Jesus, what a thing to say,' I replied. 'Of course not. She wouldn't leave us.'

But I was mad angry by then that Danny – and all of us – were having to go through all this. In many ways it was harder for us older kids because we'd known Mammy when she was a proper mother. Danny and Paul, the two youngest, had really only ever had a drunk for a mother.

I needed someone to blame. And the obvious person was Daddy's bit on the side. Back then, in my mind, it seemed that before she appeared on the scene, everything had been fine. Without her, my family would still be happy, my mammy would still be sober. The more I thought about it, the more angry I became. I wanted to kill her for what she'd done, all the pain she had caused. Looking back now I know it was just as much Daddy's fault; she was just a kid, but then I hated her.

I talked to anyone I knew who I thought might tell me what had been going on between Daddy and this woman. Gradually I pieced the information together and worked out that Daddy's girlfriend was just a year older than me – and younger than Bridget! There were rumours she called him her sugar daddy because he'd buy her anything that she wanted. Oh, and also, she had a young daughter, who by then was about three years old – just 18 months older than his own granddaughter, Sarah-Jane. When I heard that I felt sick to my stomach. Maybe Mammy had been right all along about Daddy's mistress carrying his baby.

I decided to have it out with the woman – it was the way traveller women dealt with things.

One lunchtime, I went to the pub where she and Daddy used to drink together. Quite a lot of travellers went in there and the bar staff were friendly but they didn't know me as Tommy's daughter because I'd never been in before.

I started chatting to the young fella behind the bar. 'I've got some old clothes for big Tommy's girlfriend,' I said. 'Do you know where she lives?'

He waved towards a block of flats on the estate. 'She's in there,' he said.

'OK, thanks,' I said, slowly finishing my glass of Coke before setting off home. When I got back the house was empty. The little 'uns and Sarah-Jane were either at school or round at Bridget's.

I knew exactly what I was going to do and felt incredibly calm as I did it. I pulled my big old suitcase out of the loft and packed clothes for Sarah-Jane and all my brothers and sisters, their favourite toys, drinking cups, bottles and a couple of family snaps. Then in a smaller rucksack I put just a few of my clothes and a picture of me, Bridget and the kids.

I put them both in the hall by the front door, tidied up the kitchen, mopped the floor then locked the back door.

I needed everything sorted and tidy because I didn't think I'd be coming back for a long while. The kids' clothes were so they could move back in with Bridget. Mine were for when I was in prison.

My plan was set. I was going to go round to her house and knock seven bells out of her. If that meant doing jail, I was ready for it.

Looking back, I was like a woman possessed. I think years of seeing my family gradually fall apart had finally got to me. I wanted revenge. But at the time I felt totally in control, as if I was doing the most normal thing in the world.

Half an hour later I was outside the flats that the barman had pointed out, staring at about a hundred buzzers with no idea which one to press. I hung around outside until someone finally came out and I described the girl I was looking for. He directed me to the third flat along on the second floor.

I strode up the steps and walked along the corridor until I found the door. I banged on the reinforced glass and waited.

The second the door swung open and the girl with peroxide hair saw me she instantly set it flying shut again, bolting it immediately. She obviously knew exactly who I was.

I was pissed off already but that sent me into a full-on rage. I started kicking and slamming my fists into the door as hard as I could. 'Come out of there,' I was screaming. 'I know what you've done.'

I was raging like a mad woman but I could hear her shouting out to me from behind the bolted door. 'It's not me, it's him,' she was screaming. 'I tell him to go back to his wife and kids but he won't. He swore to me on his mammy's grave that he loves me and he will never leave me.'

All us travellers had been brought up believing that country people had lower moral standards than travellers but surely even this woman could see what she was doing was just too cruel. Hearing her excuses just sent me even more crazy. I knew my daddy would never curse on his mother's grave – she had to be lying. Didn't she? Years of pent-up fury came spewing out as I slammed myself into her front door. But however hard I tried, it wouldn't budge. Tears were streaming down my face that even now I couldn't get in and show that woman what I thought about how she'd destroyed my family.

I must have been there ten minutes when a car screeched up outside the flats and two really rough-looking lads came up to the landing where I was stood. Daddy's girlfriend must have called them. They were both built like brick shit houses and were carrying baseball bats which they slammed menacingly into the palms of their free hands.

They walked towards me slowly and suddenly I felt very scared.

'Are you causing trouble girl?' one of them said in a broad Manc accent.

Although the thought of prison hadn't frightened me earlier in the day, I didn't feel quite so tough now. 'Do you know who my daddy is?' I said, knowing it was the only thing that might save me. Daddy still had connections that could put the frighteners on the toughest boys on the estate.

'I don't fucking care who he is,' one of them grunted, swinging back his baseball bat.

'Look you eedjit,' I said with far more bravery than I

actually felt by then, 'if you know her inside then you'll know she's with Big Tommy. He's my daddy and if he finds out you've laid a finger on me, your lives will be over.'

It was enough, just enough, to make them stop for a moment.

I turned and walked back along the landing, down the stairs and home. I cried all the way, tears of disappointment that I'd failed.

When I got home, Daddy was there. I went mad all over again. 'How could you have been with her?' I screamed.

'You've got the wrong end of the stick,' Daddy said, desperately trying to talk his way out of the situation.

'D'ya think we're stupid?' I screamed. 'It's been going on for years and everyone on the estate knows.'

'It's not what you think,' he replied. 'She's just a good friend of mine.'

'Really?' I said. Then I told him about all the times I'd spied on them together in the pub and how I'd just been round to her flat and she'd insisted it was him who wouldn't leave her alone!

Bridget was there too and was saying, 'Oh Daddy, you wouldn't do that, would you Daddy?'

'Yes,' I said. 'He would. He did.'

For ages Daddy didn't say anything at all. Then finally he looked up at the pair of us. 'Yes, I did,' he said. 'But she's no whore.'

Bridget was shaking and I knew she was about to start crying. I grabbed her arm and dragged her out of the house. I was so mad I didn't want him to see how much he'd hurt B. How much he'd hurt me. Daddy hadn't just cheated on Mammy, he'd smashed everything we'd ever believed in.

But weirdly, after the big confrontation, nothing actually changed. Things just carried on exactly the same. Mammy was in no fit state to throw Daddy out so he just kept on coming and going between our house and his girlfriend's flat. There was nothing we could do to stop him.

Around about then, Stevie turned up.

It was one Saturday afternoon, just after the start of *Grandstand*, when he just banged on the door, carrying a holdall over his shoulder.

'It's great to see you, Rosie,' he said, stepping straight into the hall and throwing himself down on the sofa in the living room.

'Where the hell have you been?' I shouted. 'And if you don't recognise the baby sat there on the rug, that's your daughter.'

'Ain't she beautiful,' he said, picking her up and sitting her on his knee. Sarah-Jane wasn't remotely scared of the big stranger who'd just walked in the room. In fact, she seemed quite mesmerised by him. She was always a daddy's girl.

'So,' I repeated. 'Where have you been?'

'Working in London,' he said.

'Working?' I screamed. 'For eight months? That'd be a first! And don't they have telephones in London?'

'Ah, leave it Rosie,' he said, going upstairs and running the bath.

And that was it. The end of the conversation. Stevie just drifted back into our life as effortlessly as he had drifted out. In our culture you marry for life and I had been brought up to believe there was no other option. He was my husband however he behaved and that was that.

We got back into some kind of routine of married life but still Stevie's disappearances continued. Sometimes it'd just be for a night when he was out on a bender with his mates. Other times it'd be the whole weekend or anything up to a fortnight.

I let him get on with whatever it was he was doing because I couldn't really see any alternative. I'd made my bed and I was having to lie in it. That was the traveller way. And yes, I guess part of me kept hoping Stevie would change and become the husband and father to our daughter that I dreamed of. Divorce was not an option and after all, he was still the father of my child.

So instead of worrying about Stevie, I tried to focus all my efforts on my younger brothers and sisters and Sarah-Jane. I was determined to give them as normal a childhood as possible. At weekends me and Bridget would take them to the park or the cinema then get home in time for a big stew, just like the ones Mammy had made when I was little. During the week I made sure all the kids were up, washed and in school on time. When they got home in the evening there was no television until they'd done their homework and before bed I'd listen to the younger ones read their stories. Sometimes I could only pick out a couple of words myself in their beginners' reading books but I made them carry on anyway, both of us sounding out words together slowly if we didn't instantly recognise them.

My education had been such a mess, pulled from school to school and barely learning a thing along the way, that it made me determined that Sarah-Jane and my brothers and sisters would have better. When we went into town I'd ask them to read me the shop signs to practise their letters and

I'd make up stories in my head then get them to write them out. I did everything I could to help them learn.

I desperately wanted the little kids to have the chance of a better life, a life like the one I'd once dreamed about. I particularly didn't want the girls, Tina, Maria and my Sarah-Jane to have a life of cooking, cleaning and being hooked up with a man who didn't give a damn about anything other than partying. In other words, a life like mine.

14

Always Waiting

I was waiting for him to come back. Again.

I was always waiting for Stevie. He was still disappearing for weeks or months on end, leaving me at home alone, never knowing when he would reappear through the door as if he'd just been down the shops for a packet of fags.

He knew the moment he returned there'd be an almighty great row but he also knew that as a traveller woman I could never turn him away. Like all traveller women I was a wife for life. So sure enough, after a couple of days of shouting and screaming at each other, Stevie would soon have his feet back under the table and his flabby white backside in my bed.

Sarah-Jane was coming up for two and saying her first few words when Stevie decided we should go back to Germany again.

'My cousin says there's loads of work out there again at the moment and we should go over,' he said.

I'd long since stopped believing that Stevie would go anywhere because he was desperate to work. More likely he just wanted to be out and about drinking and partying with his cousins again.

'But what about little Danny and the others?' I said. Sean and Tommy were out working with Daddy then and Tina and Maria were 14 and 13, but they still weren't old enough to look after themselves. Jimmy was eleven and just starting big school, Pauly was nine and Danny was seven but because of his learning disabilities he still needed constant care.

None of that mattered to Stevie.

'They can stay with Bridget,' he said. 'Anyway, you're my wife, you should be coming with me.'

I suppose I could have refused and stayed put but then his whole family would have taken against me for being a bad wife. And part of me kept on hoping that if we could find somewhere where Stevie was truly happy then he'd stick around and we could finally be a proper family.

Bridget was in floods of tears when I went round to say goodbye. 'Will ya' be alright?' she said.

'Of course, I'll be just grand,' I replied. But in truth I had no idea how our trip would turn out.

It was agonising saying goodbye to Danny again. I hated leaving him even more than I had the last time. It wasn't like things had got any better at home. I felt awful.

'Now you be a good fella for B,' I told him, kissing his cheeks till they turned red.

'I'm always good, me,' he replied. He was such a cheeky little thing by then.

'Really?' I tried to laugh. 'Well I'd better be on the phone twice a day just to check you are then,' I said. 'And I'll be back soon too so you'll have me to answer to if you're naughty.'

I really didn't know when we would be back but I hoped it wouldn't be too long. I couldn't bear the thought of Danny growing up without me. But I had to give this a go for the sake of Sarah-Jane and my marriage. It felt like our last chance.

So we set off again back to Germany. We flew out there

then stayed in a trailer belonging to one of Stevie's cousins. It was a two-bedroom trailer and it had been decked out quite nicely with red striped curtains and a beige sofa in the living area.

Sarah-Jane was happy to potter around from room to room but I soon felt like me and her were virtual prisoners in that trailer.

The site where we were living was almost entirely made up of Stevie's relatives and although they were generally good people and the women were polite to me, it wasn't the same as having my own family around. I felt like I was never included if there was a party going on or if everyone was going out. I was always hanging around the edges and if the other women were going out shopping they rarely asked me to join them.

I spent more and more time alone in the trailer with Sarah-Jane. I was lonely and miserable. And although I'd always been slim, my weight dropped even further until I was a scrawny size six. I lost all interest in food. I'd lost interest in most things really apart from Sarah-Jane.

Stevie was of course back to his old ways. At the time there was a big rave scene going on in the area where we were living and Stevie and his mates were really into it. I'd got used to him drinking but I became worried that he'd get involved with all the drugs that I knew got passed around at raves. 'Please don't go out tonight,' I'd beg him.

But he wouldn't listen. 'Just leave it,' came his familiar response time and time again. If I persisted, there would be a quick slap to shut me up. He wasn't one of those men who'd batter me after a night out drinking so that I'd end up in hospital. He preferred to just hand out quick slaps any time that he felt I was threatening his authority.

They still hurt of course but more than anything they were humiliating, a constant reminder that what I thought and felt really didn't matter one bit.

Sometimes his mates would come round and they would openly take the mickey out of me. Stevie's mate Mikey would come round to our trailer and the pair of them would get themselves showered and dressed for a night out, splashing on the aftershave and gelling their hair. 'It's going to be a good night at that club,' I heard Mikey laugh once. 'There'll be plenty of pures there, better lookers than this ol' one you've got here.'

'Pures' is a traveller word for women. I knew that must be what they were out doing. I felt utterly humiliated but I didn't know what to do about it. I still didn't know for absolutely certain that he was cheating on me but I didn't have to be a genius to see the signs. But it was different to a country woman finding out her husband was womanising. There was nothing I could do even if he was, so I might as well just put it out of my mind. Whatever he did, and whoever he did it with, Stevie was my husband and that wasn't going to change.

'You want to lose that ball and chain,' his mate Mikey said to him in front of me another time.

'Shut it,' replied Stevie. But deep down I reckon he thought Mikey was right. Oh I was useful to him, to wash his shirts, cook his meals and to sleep with him. But beyond that I was nothing but an irritation.

When Stevie and his mates went out, some of their wives would go too. 'Maybe I could get someone to mind

Sarah-Jane and come out too,' I'd say sometimes. 'Some of the other girls are going so I wouldn't be in your way.'

'Nah,' he'd reply. 'Not tonight. You stay here in case the baby needs you.'

And like in England, he often went missing for days at a time. I didn't know if he was drinking, taking drugs or staying with another woman. I stopped asking and tried not to think about it. Nothing that I said or thought was going to change anything.

'If you give me the money for a flight I'll go home and get out of your way,' I said to Stevie one night.

'You will not,' he replied. 'You're my wife and you're staying here with me.'

And that was the end of it.

I couldn't really understand it. He clearly didn't love me any more, if he had ever loved me in the first place. But he couldn't let me go either. I was stuck in a no man's land and was becoming lonelier and more depressed by it all with every day that passed.

One night, as he stood in front of the mirror, combing his hair ready to go out, I felt I couldn't stand it any longer. 'I don't want you going out again,' I said. 'I'm thousands of miles from home, surrounded by your family not mine, I've got a toddler to look after and I'm knackered. I'm lonely here on my own night after night. I want you to stay with me.'

'Well I don't want to be anywhere near you,' he snarled.

I could feel the tears welling in my eyes but I wasn't going to back down now. 'Well fuck you,' I replied. 'Daddy was right about you all along. You're bad news.'

That was it. I felt his fist smash into my face and could feel something damp running down my chin. Blood.

But rather than back down like I'd done all those times before, this time the pain just fired me on. 'Just one?' I screamed. 'Just one black eye? Go on, do the other one. Be a real man and finish the job off, punch me in the left eye too.'

Stevie was enraged but must have felt he couldn't hit me again now I was goading him to do it. 'Come on then,' I kept yelling. 'Aren't ya man enough to do it twice?'

He didn't even look to see the damage he'd caused. He just spun round and stormed out of the trailer.

I'd had enough. I didn't sleep a wink. First thing the next morning I strapped Sarah-Jane in her buggy and pushed her to the phone box by the dual carriageway near our site.

I typed in the number that I knew off by heart and felt a surge of relief when I heard a voice at the other end.

'Hello Daddy,' I said. 'I want to come home. Can you help me?'

Daddy didn't ask a single question about what had been happening, he simply issued his instructions and made everything OK. 'Get your things, go to the airport and call me again from there. I'll get down to the travel agent and book you on a flight now. You'll be home by tonight.'

It was all I'd wanted to hear.

I went back to the trailer and put all mine and the baby's things into one holdall. I popped into Stevie's cousin Gina's trailer and explained what I was doing.

'I don't blame ya doll,' she said, giving me a hug.

I couldn't write well enough to leave a note and Stevie wouldn't have been able to read it even if I could.

I had just enough money in my purse left over from the previous day's food shopping to get us a cab to the airport. Daddy picked me up at the airport in Manchester.

As I walked out of the arrivals gate, carrying our battered holdall and pushing Sarah-Jane in her buggy, I could see him staring at me. He looked horrified.

'You OK, Rosie?' he said.

'Yeah, I'm just grand,' I replied. I shot him a thin smile and a look that he understood immediately: Don't ask me anything, Daddy. Just pretend everything is normal and then maybe, just maybe, I'll get through this.

'Good, well if you're sure,' he said.

Then he picked Sarah-Jane out of her buggy and threw her high up into the air in the middle of the airport terminal.

'Daddy!' I laughed, as Sarah-Jane giggled hysterically. 'What?' he joked. 'Am I not supposed to be glad to see my two little girls?' Sarah-Jane was still giggling but I saw the strain on Daddy's face.

When I nipped to the toilets in the arrivals hall I could see why he'd looked so upset. My eye was swollen and a deep shade of blue and there were still specks of dried blood around my nose.

But Daddy didn't say a thing about it from that moment on. I didn't want to go through the whole thing again with him. We both knew the reality of what had happened but what good could talking do now? My marriage was a disaster but I was married for life – those were the rules. And although I know Daddy would have been steaming mad about Stevie hurting me, he was just glad that for the time being I was a long way away from him and out of harm's way.

I was so relieved to be home. But still there was never any question things were over permanently between me and Stevie. I knew he'd be back. He'd always be back, when it suited him. I just had to wait for whenever that would be.

When we got back to our house, Mammy was there and surprisingly she was fairly sober. 'What's that bastard done to your face?' she asked, the moment she opened the door.

'Ah nothing,' I replied. 'I did it to meself.' It was a totally idiotic thing to say and I knew she wouldn't believe it for a moment but I still felt loyalty to Stevie. He was my husband after all. And I didn't want to admit that Mammy and Daddy had been right about him all along.

Me and Sarah-Jane settled back into life with Mammy and Daddy but a couple of months later, sure enough, Stevie was back.

'I'm sorry Rosie,' he said. 'I'm sorry about everything. I love you. Let's get back together. It'll be different now, I'll get a job and we could have another baby. I'll stop partying, it'll all be fine.'

I never for one moment believed it wouldn't happen again. I always thought it probably would. But Stevie had the charm and the chat so I took him back. And what choice did I really have but to take him back? I couldn't divorce him, I'd be ostracised by the traveller community – my friends and my family – forever if I did that. Looking back I can see that probably my family would have come to terms with it if they felt it was my only way of being safe. But back then I was so conditioned by traveller thinking that I was convinced I'd never be forgiven. I told myself that my only option was to hope the good times lasted a little longer this time and grit my teeth when they came to an end.

Daddy knew I had to take Stevie back but he was still furious with him. 'You touch my little girl one more time and I'll beat you till you can't stand up,' he threatened Stevie.

'I won't Sir,' Stevie replied. I don't think Daddy believed

his promises any more than I did. But Daddy was as hide-bound by traveller conventions as I was and despite everything he'd done himself he still believed a wife's place was with her husband.

Me, Stevie and Sarah-Jane stayed near Mammy and Daddy's house in our trailer and I saw them and my brothers and sisters most days. At first Stevie did seem a changed character and every morning he'd get himself washed and showered and be out the door by six o'clock to the building site where he'd picked up work.

Two months after his return from Germany I was pregnant again. Traveller women weren't supposed to use birth control, so if it was God's will you should fall pregnant, then so be it. Maybe the opposition to using contraception was partly because we were Catholic but there was also a feeling among traveller women that birth control was for country women. For traveller women, the only man you'd ever sleep with would be your husband and any child that came from that was regarded a blessing.

I was pleased at the thought of having another baby and a playmate for Sarah-Jane. But I was barely four months gone when I became worried that Stevie was slipping back into his old ways, going for a few drinks after work, then staying out till the early hours, then disappearing for nights on end. Soon he lost his job and then he was nicking my child benefit money to go out partying. We couldn't speak to each other without rowing and then of course his way of shutting me up was still a slap across the face. It was all so depressingly familiar.

By the time our second child, Tyrone, was born in May 1991, we were separated again. After one enormous great bust-up he'd stormed out of the trailer and I'd heard he was living with one of his cousins over in Huddersfield. The baby was just a couple of days old when he reappeared with a bunch of sick-looking roses for me and the usual selection of promises that he'd change and could we just give it one more go.

And so we did. Yeh, it was the same old story.

When Stevie wasn't drinking he was the best father in the world. He was funny and charming, would play with the kids and even sometimes cook me romantic meals, well, empty takeaway cartons onto a plate, anyway. He was still good looking and charming and I felt he could probably have any woman he wanted but still he kept coming back to me. And in my mind, back then, that meant something. Part of me knew that he just wanted me to be his skivvy but I managed to convince myself that each time he came back to me it must mean he loved me really.

And at times it really seemed like he did.

For weeks on end after one of our reunions he'd come back with bunches of flowers for me every night, until I didn't have vases to put them in. And they weren't those cheap ones you get in cellophane from petrol stations either.

One evening I was cooking our tea when he came up behind me at the cooker and put his arms around my waist.

'I've got a surprise for you,' he said seriously. 'It's a ring. Don't go mad at me spending so much money on it. I wanted to do it for you.'

He gently pulled my arm behind my back and slipped the ring on my third finger. I lifted it up to look at it and instantly started laughing. 'Another bloody cracker ring!' I yelled.

'Well, you liked the first one so much, I thought I'd get you another,' he said, that cheeky grin back on his face the way it had been in the early days.

He could still make me laugh. If only he hadn't made me cry so many times over the years.

But Stevie could never steer clear of bad company. The people he sought out for his mates were always the drinkers and the men who'd barely done a day's work in their lives. But he loved the craic of being with them and got swept along in the drinking and partying.

And so on and on it went in the same way. We were married for almost five years without spending a single anniversary together!

It felt like such an event that we were still together as we approached our fifth wedding anniversary that we decided to celebrate it by getting our marriage blessed by a priest in the church. In the eyes of the Catholic Church that meant we would finally be properly wed.

I went to Mass at the church every Sunday morning and I took it very seriously that Stevie and I would be exchanging our vows in the eyes of God. We attended marriage classes for four weeks before the service and I prayed that this was what might give our marriage a new lease of life. Stevie was still going out partying but not so often at that point and I hoped maybe he really was serious about making things work. Other people were less convinced.

One morning after Mass, the priest called me to one side. 'So, all set for next Saturday then, Rosie?' he asked.

'Yes, Father, thank you,' I replied.

'You know,' he said slowly. 'You don't have to go through

with this. If you don't feel he is the husband you want, you don't have to marry him.'

I couldn't believe a priest was suggesting this when we were already married legally, if not in the eyes of God. But I knew he only had my best interests at heart; he'd seen me when I'd turned up at Mass with slap marks on my face or when Stevie had gone off and left me again.

'Oh no, Father,' I said. 'It'll be fine.'

But within days of our blessing, Stevie was back preening himself in front of the mirror for another big night out, goodness knows where and with goodness knows who.

One morning I woke up with a terrible itching and burning sensation between my legs. I was desperate to pee but when I tried, nothing came out. It was the kind of thing that traveller women would never talk about so I tried to ignore it, hoping it might just go away. But after three or four days it was just becoming more and more painful. I went to the GP who examined me down below.

'Now, Rosie,' she said. 'How many sexual partners have you had?'

I nearly swung for the snooty old cow. 'I'm a married woman,' I said.

'Anything you tell me in here is confidential,' she went on. 'It's between me and you, so tell me, how many men have you slept with?'

Was this woman calling me a whore? 'I have slept with my husband and that is it,' I snapped.

'OK,' she said, suddenly looking a little awkward. 'Well you have a Sexually Transmitted Disease – the only way you could have caught that is from having slept with someone infected with the disease.'

I stared at her, really not sure what she was trying to tell me.

She carried on talking quickly. 'What I'm concerned about is that the disease appears to have travelled to the neck of your womb. We need to admit you to hospital for treatment if we're going to prevent permanent damage.'

I had to go straight into the hospital for tests and treatment and it was only later that I sat back and thought about what the doctor had said. If I'd caught this disease from Stevie, then where had he caught it from? It was no real surprise to work out that he'd been sleeping around. I suppose deep down I'd always known it. But to discover it for certain in such a horrible way was sickening. He wasn't even around at that time to row with about it.

'He's never going to change, is he Mammy?' I asked one day when she was sitting on the couch, more sober than usual.

'No, Rosie,' she said. 'But as I always told you, you have to stop fighting and do things the traveller way – and that means being married for life no matter what happens.' And Mammy was a woman who'd been sent to the deepest depths of alcoholism by a cheating husband, and was still married. How could I possibly do things differently? But it worried me when I looked at my own daughter. This certainly wasn't the kind of marriage and life that I'd want her to have.

I began to think seriously about how I might be able to give my kids a different life. I spent hours working out how I could buy our own house. Not a trailer where we were always moving from place to place, always looking for the perfect spot which never quite existed. And not even a rented house where you could be turfed out whenever the landlord wanted. No, I decided I wanted to buy our own place where we could stay forever. We could paint the walls and I'd buy lemon curtains for the kitchen windows. The kids could have their own bedrooms where they would be able to keep their schoolbooks without them getting tatty or covered in food stains from the kitchen. They'd be able to go to the same school with no interruptions and make friends that they'd stay near for the rest of their lives. Then when they grew up they would be able to go out and explore the world but they'd always have a home to come back to. And we'd be happy there.

That became my dream. As to how to achieve it, I really wasn't sure.

My first ambition was to get my kids the very best education I possibly could. I heard about a private nursery near where we were living and decided that was where Sarah-Jane was going to go, no matter what the cost. I rang up the nursery and they said there was a place available. 'I'll take it,' I said, without even asking about the cost.

Then I went round to Daddy. 'Please,' I begged. 'I want to do things right by Sarah-Jane – will you pay for her to go to nursery?'

Daddy was still doing well, buying and selling scrap, and he could afford the fees so he agreed. Soon Sarah-Jane was learning her ABC and playing with children from all kinds of backgrounds. I was amazed how quickly children could learn when they were in a stable, secure environment. But that made me sad when I thought about the pitiful state of my own reading and writing. My whole education consisted of nothing but missed opportunities.

15

Life Goes On

Mammy's drinking went in fits and starts. Sometimes she'd be able to talk quite normally and even play with the youngest kids, Danny and Pauly. But other times she'd be totally out of it, back with her street-drinking pals, swigging vodka out of the bottle on a park bench.

Every couple of months we'd get Daddy to take her off to a cousin's for a few days then Bridget and I would clean the house from top to bottom. I'd paint some of the rooms because there was no other way of getting the thick smoke stains off the wall. But as soon as she got home it immediately started returning to filth again.

A couple of times Daddy took her away in the trailer and camped up in the middle of nowhere, thinking that she wouldn't be able to get hold of alcohol there and could dry out. But she was so determined. She'd slip out while he was asleep, then walk for miles to buy booze at an off-licence or corner shop.

Nothing we could think of would keep her away from alcohol.

Then, in the summer of 1992, she hit rock bottom. She was having drastic mood swings and became really nasty for no particular reason. She banned me from going round to clean the house or even visiting her at home. 'Get out.

Out,' she'd said. 'It is clean enough around here, I don't need you sticking your nose in.'

But Mammy wasn't taking any care of herself and was putting herself in daily danger, falling asleep holding lighted cigarettes, not eating, and drinking anything at all that she thought might get her drunk.

We tried to persuade her to go into hospital to get proper psychiatric help for her alcoholism to give her a chance of getting better once and for all.

She wouldn't hear of such a thing. 'There's nothing wrong with me,' she'd rant at us. 'All I need is to be left alone.'

But we couldn't leave her alone. More and more often we'd find her paralytic on one of the wooden benches in the city centre or lying asleep in a park near our house. We pulled her out of gutters, picked her up in alleyways and dragged her out of pubs. Twice she got into the car and started driving even though she was so drunk she couldn't see where she was going. Once she drove straight into a row of parked cars. When police pulled her out of the driving seat she couldn't stand up. We were terrified she might do it again at any moment and kill either herself or someone else.

No matter how hard we tried we couldn't keep her away from drink.

Once, I was staying over and I woke up in the morning to find she'd taken my jeans from the side of my bed. I guess she wanted the cash in my pockets but she took the jeans as well! She would nick anything that she could to the pawnshop for a couple of quid. Piece by piece, all her beloved Crown Derby ended up there. Then we noticed that her engagement and wedding rings were missing too. Her wedding ring had been handmade and was absolutely beautiful. It had cost Daddy thousands of pounds and we knew Mammy would have sold it for a fraction of that.

Me and Bridget stomped down to the pawn shop and saw it right there, in a glass case in the shop window.

'Did you buy these rings off our mammy when you could see she had a drink problem?' I demanded of the fella behind the counter, pointing at the rings.

'She wasn't drunk when she came in here,' the shop manager replied, all smug.

'Really? Well I bet she bloody well was half an hour later,' I snapped, handing over £200 to buy them back.

We took the rings home and hid them. We couldn't trust Mammy with her own rings any more but we didn't want a stranger to have them either. Soon after that we came home and found the television had gone missing. Then it was the microwave and even some of her half-empty bottles of perfume, which despite once being really expensive can only have earned her coins.

Mammy was barred from every shop and pub in the area for drunkenness and shoplifting. Sean and Tommy were keeping well out of the way most of the time now, staying round at friends' houses whenever they could. But Tina, Maria, Jimmy and Pauly were all mortified that their mother was known as the local drunk. Poor Danny had never known any different and because of his learning difficulties he didn't understand why his mammy was different. But sometimes he'd play at being Mammy, putting on a slurred voice and dragging his leg as he walked along like she did when she couldn't stand up. It was pitiful and heartbreaking to watch.

Mammy was becoming more and more out of control and we were terrified that if we really did leave her alone it would only be a matter of weeks until she was dead.

Me and Bridget often followed her to see where she was getting money from to buy the booze and who was serving it to her. We'd stay a fair distance behind her and hide behind cars and bushes if she ever looked round. But she barely knew where she was going herself.

We caught her twice in a supermarket. Once we watched totally astonished as she walked around the store pushing a half-full trolley of groceries and looking for all the world like any other customer. Except she'd swiped a bottle of vodka off one of the shelves and every time she was in an empty aisle she was glugging it back. When she'd finished she simply hid the empty bottle behind some cereal boxes, abandoned her shopping trolley and walked boldly out of the supermarket. Me and Bridget couldn't believe it. We had to stop it happening again though so we told the security guard who stopped her and she was arrested.

I felt sick when she was carted off in a police car but it was the only way I could be sure that she wouldn't be allowed in the supermarket again to do the same thing.

Another time it was nearly midnight when Mammy slipped out of the house. We heard the front door click on the latch and me and Bridget were after her in a flash. We followed her quietly down the road but she must have clocked us somehow because suddenly she turned round.

'Where are yous going?' she said to me and Bridget.

'Just out for some fags,' we replied.

She spun round again and carried on walking, but wherever she went, we followed. Then she reached a T-junction ahead of us and turned left. But by the time we got to the junction she had totally disappeared. We couldn't understand where she could have gone to – the only way she could have slipped out of view would be if she was hiding in someone's garden.

'Where the hell is she?' we kept saying as we peered through bushes and over garden walls. Twenty minutes went by and we couldn't see her anywhere. We were about to give up and go home when I heard a rattling sound further down the road. I looked down the street and saw the metal lid of a dustbin was raised slightly in the air and underneath it two little eyes were peering out. She'd only gone and hidden in a bloody bin!

'What the hell are you doing, Mammy?' I said. 'Get yourself out of there.'

It sounds funny but it really wasn't. We dragged her out and took her home. She was kicking and screaming all the way, complaining that we were making her life a misery.

But as far as we were concerned we were the only thing keeping her alive. We were constantly on the hunt for her hidden stash of alcohol in the house. Most of it was so well hidden we never found it but if we did find a half-full bottle of vodka inside the toilet cistern or under the sofa cushions we'd tip most of it out and replace it with water. We thought that was safest because if we just threw the whole bottle away she'd only go out and get another one.

I was literally making myself sick with worry. I couldn't sleep at night thinking that she'd be wandering the streets and was about to get run over or attacked or choke on her

own vomit. Me, Stevie and the kids had moved into a council house down the road by then. The little 'uns divided
their time between me and Bridget's, and first thing each
morning I'd be straight round to Mammy's to check she
was safely in bed. Then I'd come back and get the kids
ready for school, make breakfast for them and tidy up the
house. And all the time, all I'd be able to think about was
what Mammy might be doing to herself. My weight
plummeted.

One night she rolled home and fell into such a deep sleep
that me and Bridget were convinced she was in a coma.

'She's really dying this time,' I screamed at Bridget. 'Call
an ambulance.'

When Mammy came to and realised what we were doing,
she started screaming so much that Bridget and I had to
wrap her in a sheet like an Egyptian mummy then carry her
out to the ambulance.

At hospital the doctors examined her then called me and
Bridget into a side room.

'Your mother's condition is extremely serious,' the
doctor said. 'If she carries on drinking at this level she will
die. We think she should be sectioned under the Mental
Health Act for her own safety.'

We knew that meant she would be kept in hospital,
against her will if necessary, until she was no longer a
danger to herself. To me, the idea came as a huge relief.
She'd be somewhere safe and hopefully a long way away
from alcohol. When she came round we couldn't bring
ourselves to tell her that she'd been sectioned though, we
knew she'd be furious.

A couple of days later I went in to visit Mammy and as

soon as I arrived at the bottom of the bed, she said, 'Ah Rosie, I'm so glad you're here. Get my clothes out of that cupboard over there. I'm going home.'

'You can't go home, Mammy,' I said quietly.

'Of course I can,' she replied. 'I've had enough of this place.'

'No Mammy, you can't. It's the law. You've been sectioned.'

At that she went completely crazy at me. 'I've been sectioned? Is this your idea?'

'We've had to do it,' I said. 'It's for your own good,' I tried to explain.

'For your good, you mean,' she snapped. 'It's just you and your daddy wanting to keep me out of the way so he can get on with his fancy woman.'

At that, Mammy ran out into the corridor and tried to grab coats from the back of chairs that people had left during visiting time. When she got to the end of the corridor she started banging on the door. But it was locked with a security guard the other side and there was no way of escaping. When she realised there was no way out she started sobbing like a child. She was so desperate to get away, so desperate for a drink, but there was nothing we could do.

With Mammy in hospital I cleaned her house out all over again. Daddy was officially still living there but we all knew he was rarely at home. I threw out furniture and carpets and painted the whole lot. But every room I went into I found more and more empty bottles of vodka. They were under the kitchen units, under floorboards and stuffed up chimney breasts. Mammy had even safety-pinned Daddy's socks into the linings of the curtains then stashed a bottle in each sock. It was so clever, but so tragic, at the same time. There was even a bottle inside a glass chandelier in the front room.

It took days for the stench of vomit and piss to fade away but gradually it looked and smelt clean again.

Mammy had been in hospital for about three weeks when one morning a visitor for another patient came in and somehow, no one ever did explain to us how, Mammy slipped out of the door. She went totally unnoticed from the ward and was into the hospital grounds when a nurse who'd been treating her spotted her there. The nurse didn't have a mobile phone on her and didn't want to stop to raise the alarm in case she lost sight of Mammy so instead she followed her on foot.

By then Mammy weighed little more than six stone but that morning she walked the full seven miles back home without even pausing for breath. By the time she reached the end of the road, the nurse was struggling to keep up and was totally knackered. But Mammy appeared to have boundless energy. She dived into the corner shop at the end of our road, reappeared with a bottle of vodka and went straight home.

Seeing where Mammy had gone the nurse was able to ring her boss at the hospital who then called me. I went straight round to the house and together me and the nurse bundled Mammy back into my car just as she was opening her bottle of vodka. She fought like fury to stop us taking her away again. She scratched and punched and bit us but we couldn't let her stay.

Even though I knew hospital was the best place for Mammy, I still felt terribly guilty for shutting her away. She begged us to let her stay at home and it was heartbreaking. I worried about it all the time and it made me feel very low. On top of that I was still looking after my own kids, my brothers and sisters, and cooking and washing for Daddy too. He'd been good to me since I moved back to England but I was still mad at him for having the affair. In my mind that was still at the root of all our family's troubles.

Stevie was back to coming and going whenever he fancied.

All in all, I was exhausted. I was still just 22 years old but I felt like an old woman. The stresses of the past years had taken their toll on me. I was barely eating or sleeping, I was feeling weepy all the time and just didn't have the energy to keep fighting. I took myself off to my GP and told him I was feeling a little under the weather.

'It's nothing much, I'm just a bit tired,' I said, not really wanting to make much of a fuss.

'Well, has much been happening at home lately?' he asked.

'Oh, only me husband running off, me daddy having an affair and me mammy being sectioned for alcoholism,' I laughed. 'And I've got seven kids to look after.'

'I see,' he said.

Twenty minutes later I was on my way with a prescription for anti-depressants and the telephone number for the Samaritans.

I took the anti-depressants for a couple of weeks but I didn't think they helped me at all. I didn't feel quite so low any more, but I didn't feel happy either. In fact I felt nothing at all. It was like the pills had completely numbed me and I hated that. I always knew that the only thing that could really get me back on my feet was me. I had to drag myself up all over again. So that was what I tried to do. It wasn't easy but thankfully I never needed that number for the Samaritans.

One evening my cousin Brian and his wife, Liz, asked me to join them for a few drinks at the local pub. Sarah-Jane and Tyrone went to stay with my brothers and sisters round at Bridget's and I decided to go out and try to forget everything that was going on.

When I went out with Brian and Liz I'd always feel a little jealous. They were so together, the way a married couple ought to be. I couldn't help but compare their marriage with the way things had turned out in mine. A lot of the time by then I felt very lonely. Stevie was always out doing his own thing, Mammy was lost to me and I knew the rift between me and Daddy would never be properly resolved while he had his 'other woman'. But in all that time I had never looked at another man. I rarely got the chance because I hardly ever went out. But even if a fella had started chatting me up, there was no way I would show any interest. Travellers would never ever get over a woman cheating on her husband. No matter what my husband got up to on his nights away from home, I could never forget I was 'a wife for life'.

It was the fact that I was incredibly loyal that made what happened that night so unfair.

When Liz got up to dance at the disco in the pub, I stayed sat at the table chatting with Brian. We'd known each other since we were kids and could have a right giggle together.

Then, at around midnight, I set off home. I went round the back of our house and immediately thought it was

strange because the door was already open and I was sure I
had locked it. Inside, in the darkness, Stevie was sitting in
an armchair next to the fireplace. He'd not been home for
a couple of weeks and he was unshaven and dirty.

'Where the hell have you been?' he snarled. I knew
instantly he'd been drinking and I was going to get hit.
There was no doubt in my mind.

'I've been for a drink with Brian and Liz,' I said, going
straight for the staircase in the hope that keeping a distance
between us might save me a beating.

'No, you fucking haven't,' he yelled.

I was already half-way up the stairs to bed.

'You've been in the pub with a man,' he went on. 'You
were seen.'

I knew better than to argue and explain that the man
was actually my cousin, and his wife had only ever been
a few yards away. I just kept on walking up the stairs,
hoping that once I was out of his sight he might calm
down a bit.

I took my clothes off and laid down under the duvet.

I'd been there less than five minutes when the bedroom
door flung open. Stevie stormed into the room, raging.
'You whore,' he yelled. 'Who is he? Who've you been with?'
He punched me hard on the side of my head then pulling
back the duvet he lifted his boot and kicked me again and
again in my legs and belly.

I remember being relieved that the kids weren't at home
and they wouldn't wake up and hear what was going on.
Every time he kicked me there was a loud thud. My head
was pounding and it felt as though every nerve ending in
my entire body was screaming out in pain.

'Stop Stevie,' I shouted. 'Stop. I've done nothing. I was with Brian.'

'Liar,' he yelled, pounding me in the face again and again.

'I'm not lying,' I said. But I was finding it hard to speak or even breathe. I could feel myself choking and realised blood was running down the back of my throat. But still Stevie kept going, hitting and kicking me with all his strength. 'Whore, bitch, whore,' he yelled with every fresh punch.

'So this is it,' I thought. 'He's going to kill me.' My head was throbbing and my vision was blurred but I could picture clearly the scene when Bridget would come round with the kids in the morning and find me dead on the bed.

Finally exhausted, I gave up trying to defend myself and protest my innocence and just laid there as he got his rage out of his system. If I was going to die anyway what was the point in fighting any more, I thought.

Finally Stevie ran out of steam and moved back down the bed and out of the room. It hurt too much to move and all I could think about was how much I wanted to go to sleep and for everything to be over. It must have been an hour later when I returned to my senses. I was still shaking with shock and when I tried to lift my head from the pillow it felt like it was being battered all over again. I lay my head back down again and felt the dampness of blood on my pillow. I could only breathe the most shallow of breaths because my ribs hurt so much.

It was so unfair. Stevie was the one who'd been out sleeping with women and partying when all I'd ever done was clean and cook and care for the kids. I'd never even looked at another man. Then here was me taking a beating from him.

The next morning I dragged myself out of bed. I didn't dare look in the mirror but washed myself in cold water and felt the swelling around my face and jaw. Walking downstairs took an age because of the pain in my ribs.

I didn't even make myself a cup of tea but walked straight up to the church where I still went to Mass every Sunday.

I waited until the priest who'd blessed our wedding came in.

He sat next to me and I told him everything; about Mammy, about Daddy's affairs and Stevie's beatings. 'I can't carry on like this,' I said. 'I want a divorce. Is that wrong?'

There was a pause that seemed to last for ever.

'Well, you know Rosie, that the Catholic Church doesn't believe in divorce. But God doesn't believe in his children being bullied and hurt either. You've got to think about yourself and your children. If your only way of keeping them and you safe is by keeping them away from this man, then that's what you must do.'

Hearing him say that gave me a huge sense of relief. I wanted someone to tell me I wasn't wrong or evil to walk away from my marriage. And that although it might be against the traveller way, or the Catholic way, it was what I had to do.

I left the church feeling stronger than I had done in years and marched home. When I got there, Stevie was still asleep on the sofa.

I picked up his pile of clothes on the floor and threw them at him. I wasn't scared of another beating. I was too fired up to care. 'Get your clothes on and get the hell out of here,' I yelled.

This time he wasn't walking out on me and I wasn't

running away from him. For the first time, I was in control and I was throwing him out.

Stevie was so groggy from the drink that he didn't really know what was going on. But as he came round he could see the way he'd smashed up my face. Maybe that was what shamed him into leaving. Or maybe he could see how angry I was and that I really meant it this time. He quietly put on his clothes and left the house.

As he stumbled down the path I thought to myself, 'That's it. I'm not going to live like a robot any more, doing the same cooking and cleaning day after day, looking after everyone else while they do whatever they please.'

Then I got a cab up to the hospital to get myself checked out. It was agony every time I took a breath so they X-rayed me and discovered Stevie had broken three of my ribs. My nose was also broken and my cheekbone was cracked. I was covered in bruises and had two black eyes.

When Bridget brought the kids home later, Sarah-Jane looked at me and was so scared she hid behind her auntie's leg. 'What's happened Mammy?' she asked finally, staring at my face.

'Oh, Mammy fell over and knocked herself last night,' I said, trying to smile. 'I'm as bad as you falling off your bike!'

It was a few days later that I found out that a woman who'd moved in down the road had told Stevie that she'd seen me in the pub with a man she didn't recognise. And for that, I'd been beaten black and blue.

I was just recovering from that ordeal when the whole family was hit by another shock.

'I'm leaving your mammy,' Daddy announced one day. 'I

want to be with Shirley.' We'd never heard him say her name before and for a split second I wondered who Shirley was. Then it hit me, our Daddy was really going to live with *her*. I was devastated. Suddenly it wasn't an affair any more, just his bit on the side. He was going to make his home with her and the kid who by then was about six and who pretty obviously must be his. This would make it serious. I didn't think our family would ever recover from the shame. Mammy was still in the psychiatric hospital at that time and he wasn't even going to wait until she returned home to break the news.

'Oh Daddy, don't do that,' Bridget pleaded.

'I've had enough,' he said. 'I'm going and I want a divorce.'

I wasn't going to plead with him to stay. I was too angry that he'd betrayed not just Mammy but all of us.

'You'd better just go then,' I yelled at him. I'd never have dared speak to Daddy like that before but I was so angry and so hurt that I couldn't help it.

So then he was gone too. After a while we sorted it so that Sean and Tommy stayed with him and the little'uns stayed with me.

When Mammy came out of hospital Social Services found her a flat about 15 minutes away. To me, it felt like my family was being scattered to the four winds, and I hated it. But Mammy barely batted an eye when we told her that Daddy wasn't going to be living there with her any more.

Before Mammy moved into the new flat I went to visit it and was horrified. It was rank. It smelt fusty and the wallpaper was a foul brown and orange patter. I worked from six in the morning until two o'clock the following morning to wash the doors, skirting boards and windows, to paint the walls and ceilings and to clean it all through. I wanted it to feel like a home for Mammy even though after years of being surrounded by a massive family she would be living there all on her own.

In my childhood everything had been so clear-cut and certain. The rules of our community were strict but they were clear: no sex before marriage, no sex outside of marriage, no divorce, no drugs and kids respecting their parents. Now everything was turned upside down. Nothing was certain any more.

If I'd been able to look outside of my family I would have seen this was happening in other traveller families across the country. Things were changing. All the problems that came with country people's modern society were creeping into our way of life too, whether we liked it or not.

16

Lost Babies

It was the day Mammy was due to move into her new flat.

I'd been back home to pick up the few belongings that she wanted to keep with her and was driving back through the city when I felt a huge smash. A car had pulled out of a side road and gone straight into the side of my little Vauxhall Nova.

'That's all I need,' I thought, as I climbed out and exchanged numbers with the other driver. I didn't think much more of it though as I carried on to Mammy's and then climbed up the stairs to her flat carrying two big boxes full of the few ornaments and photographs she hadn't already flogged to buy booze.

I'd just stepped inside her front door when I felt the strangest sensation and could feel dampness between my legs.

I rushed into the toilet, thinking I must have been suddenly hit with a really heavy period. But somehow I knew this was more than an ordinary period. Big clots of blood were pouring out of me. After a while it eased off and I tried to put it out of my mind. I was so busy sorting out Mammy, and it was only the next day that I had time to make an appointment to see my GP. She checked me out and sent me straight to the hospital.

After a few tests the doctor came back into the room,

holding my notes and said, 'Did you know you were 16 weeks pregnant?'

I was stunned. I'd had absolutely no idea at all. My periods had been very irregular for ages, which I had put down to all the worry about Mammy and everything else that had been going on.

'So have I miscarried?' I asked.

'We think that is what is happening,' he said.

I didn't know what to think. I must have fallen pregnant the last time me and Stevie slept together before I kicked him out of the house. Now here, in the same sentence, I was being told I'd got pregnant and probably had a miscarriage. I started crying and found it hard to stop. It felt so awful to think my child might have died inside me and I hadn't even known it was there, I hadn't even acknowledged its presence. I felt guilty.

Then the doctor continued talking, 'But there is a chance that the baby may survive. We need to keep you here to monitor things and give you the best chance of avoiding a miscarriage.'

The doctors said it could have been the car accident that started off the bleeding but it could have been all sorts of other things too – there was no way we'd ever know.

I stayed in hospital for two weeks. I was constantly losing more blood but each day when they scanned me they still couldn't be entirely sure that the baby had died.

I spent my time praying for a miracle and that the baby might survive.

Then on the thirteenth day in hospital I woke up and was losing great clots of blood. I was rushed in for another scan and tests and this time all my hope ran out. My baby had died. I was taken into the operating theatre for an emergency Caesarean section to deliver the foetus. Despite having had a high level of pregnancy hormones in my body, which had made them think the foetus might still be alive, it was now clear that actually the baby had been dead for weeks and had been decaying inside me. That was what had caused all the clots. The foetus had to be removed immediately or I could suffer severe infection.

Afterwards I was sent home and told to rest. I was exhausted and could barely walk up the front path. When I got back, Mammy was at my house. I sat down and she stared at me, all cross. 'Rosie, I've come round to see you. Now are you going to make me a cup of tea or what?'

I'd just lost my baby and had been bleeding non-stop for a fortnight but all Mammy could think about was herself. If I was poorly as a child she would have wrapped me up in a quilt and given me a bottle of pop as a special treat. She'd have done anything to make me feel better. But now she was so wrapped in booze that she didn't care about anyone else.

'I'll go and put the kettle on,' I said, as I inched myself up out of a chair and shuffled into the kitchen, still in terrible pain. At that moment I wanted my mammy more than ever. And there she was in the very next room. Except, she wasn't of course, not really. Not my real mammy.

Soon after I got home from the hospital, Stevie turned up again. I'd been so determined that it was over forever when I'd thrown him out. But after losing the baby I felt lower and weaker than ever. It didn't take much effort on his part to win me back that time. But then I felt even more of a failure for giving in to him.

He came back with a sad story about how on her

deathbed his auntie had asked for me and told him to treat me well and to be a better husband. We'd both loved his auntie and foolishly I thought it might be a sign that our marriage could still work. So we tried again, but things were soon back to normal.

Mammy was soon living in the same state of squalor in her flat as she had done in her new house. Me and Bridget would go up every day to change her bedsheets because she'd almost always pee the bed. We'd get the place looking all spick and span just in time for her to do it all over again the next night.

Then one day it hit me how stupid we were being. By running around, cleaning up after her, we were enabling Mammy to carry on living this life. If we just left her to sleep in her piss-soaked sheets maybe she would take more responsibility for herself.

'We're not changing that bed and clearing up after her any more,' I told Bridget one day.

'Oh Rosie, I'm not sure,' she said. 'She's our mammy, we can't leave her like that.'

'We have to,' I replied. 'Because all we're doing is making it easy for her to live like an alcoholic – and that's not helping anyone.'

Although I sounded very determined, I really wasn't sure we were doing the right thing at all. But we'd run around Mammy for so many years, searching for her when she was lost and caring for her when she was sick and it had done no good at all. It was time for some tough love.

Some of Mammy's cousins thought we were bad daughters because we had stopped looking after her properly. But they didn't understand. She was brilliant at hiding from people how much she was drinking and she was a cunning liar. Lots of her family thought she was just a bit poorly and had daughters who simply couldn't be bothered with her. They had no idea she was necking four litres of vodka a day. If we tried to tell them, they wouldn't believe it. Oh yes, Mammy was a fantastic liar. Sometimes she'd go up to the bus stop and tell people waiting in the queue that she had a sick child but didn't have enough money for a cab to get him to hospital. She was so believable that people handed her cash, which she'd then just spend immediately in the off licence on booze.

With Stevie back on the scene, it wasn't long before I fell pregnant again. After the miscarriage I'd been desperate for another child and maybe that's one reason why I welcomed Stevie back so quickly. I wanted him to put his arms around me to tell me everything would be OK. And I wanted a baby too. When the pregnancy test showed positive I was delighted.

At first everything went well but at 18 weeks, I had a small show of blood. When they scanned me they discovered that exactly the same thing had happened all over again. The baby had been dead for several weeks already. I was devastated for a second time.

Afterwards I couldn't stop crying. I stayed in bed and would barely speak. I couldn't sleep, I didn't want to go out or even play with Sarah-Jane and Tyrone or my brothers and sisters.

A couple of months later I was pregnant again but that time it lasted just six weeks before I miscarried. I was bitterly disappointed and by then I was angry too. Why did my babies keep dying?

There was a nun who lived near us who had a reputation for being able to tell people things about their future. 'You should go and see her,' Bridget said one day.

I was reluctant. Part of me preferred to remain ignorant rather than find out more bad news. But Bridget went on and on at me about it and in the end I agreed.

The nun had a smooth round face but eyes that appeared a bit sad, as if she'd seen too much pain over the years. I told her all about what had been going on and she held my hand, squeezing it when I got to the bits I still couldn't talk about without crying.

Then we talked for ages about all sorts of things and I thought she was never going to tell me anything more interesting than how she'd known my auntie when she was a girl and didn't she have the most gorgeous black ringlets!

I was just about to walk out the door when she said, 'Trust me, Rosie, you will be pregnant again soon and no matter what anyone says it will all be fine. You'll have a beautiful, healthy little boy.'

I walked away feeling a million times better. I wasn't convinced she *would* be right but she had given me hope that she *might* be right.

My optimism came crashing down a few weeks later when I started feeling really poorly again 'down below'. I was worried it might be some after-effect of the miscarriages and went straight to the hospital.

'I'm very sorry, Mrs McKinley,' said the doctor, 'but it would appear that you have a Sexually Transmitted Disease again.'

I wasn't so naive this time and knew what had probably caused it but I still needed to be absolutely sure.

'Why would I have it?' I asked.

'Well,' the doctor said, 'it could be if you have had two or more partners.'

'Haven't,' I replied flatly.

'OK, well in that case it is most likely that your husband has. I'm sorry.'

Sorry. Yep, he was sorry. I was sorry. The only person who was never sorry, was Stevie.

I was put on really strong medication to clear up the disease but it was horrifically painful. I felt as though acid had been poured on my private parts. I had to spend two weeks in hospital before I was able to go home. When I got back there was no sign of Stevie for days – he must have known I'd be out to kill him. Finally he did turn up and acted all shocked when I told him what had been wrong with me.

'Well the doctors must be wrong,' he said. 'I swear I've never been unfaithful to you. I might not have been the best husband but I've always been true to you, Rosie,' he said.

'You're treating me like a total eedjit,' I said. 'Of course the doctors aren't wrong.'

'Oh, so you believe them over your own husband then do ya?' he went on.

He always managed to do that, to twist things to appear like I was in the wrong.

I didn't even bother to argue any more. Of course I didn't believe him. But whether I did or I didn't, it didn't matter either way. It was now crystal clear in my mind, he could do whatever he wanted and I'd still be there. Despite the priest's reassurances, I still feared I would be ostracised if I divorced Stevie. But maybe in hindsight, I was using that as an excuse not to take action. It was the mid 1990s and even some traveller couples were getting divorced by then. As for country people, they were all at it – even Charles and Di! But it was a huge risk and one I then still wasn't prepared to take. Back then virtually every single person I knew was a traveller. The only country people I ever spoke to regularly were the woman in the corner shop and teachers at the kids' school. And they weren't friends. If I was drummed out of the traveller community I would have been utterly alone.

So Stevie and I carried on living together – and sleeping together. A traveller man expects his wife to sleep with him. Life in a traveller relationship isn't like the world of those glossy magazines that country girls read. It has nothing to do with a woman getting 'in the mood' or 'feeling fulfilled in the bedroom'. If a husband comes home and wants his way with his wife, that's what he gets. It's part of the culture, the tradition. It's the way things are.

So soon after, I was pregnant again. I was terrified from the very beginning that I was going to lose this baby too. I really didn't think I could cope with the disappointment a fourth time; it would be just too much to bear.

Almost immediately, things looked bleak for the child's chances of survival. I went for the first scan and as I was lying on the bed, the lady rubbed her device over my belly and stared intently at the little screen in front of her.

I could tell by the way the frown on her face grew deeper that it wasn't good news.

'I think I'll just pop out and fetch one of my colleagues,' she said.

I lay looking at the white tiled ceiling and started to cry. 'Not again God,' I prayed. 'Please, not again.'

A doctor walked into the room and stared at the screen too. He was pointing at something to his colleague and they were nodding.

'Tell me,' I said. 'Just tell me. Has my baby gone already?'

'No,' said the more senior doctor who'd just been called in. 'No, the foetus seems fine. There is however another problem. There is a fibroid in your womb about the size of a grapefruit. Now while that on its own isn't dangerous to you, it is potentially very harmful to the baby.' He took a deep breath and went on. 'I'm sorry but there is virtually no chance you'll be able to carry this baby to full term. In this situation we recommend a termination.'

'No,' I screamed out. 'No, I won't do it. I can't do it.' Losing three babies had almost killed me, I couldn't willingly get rid of a fourth.

'Well, why don't you take some time to think about it and come back to us,' the doctor said, squeezing my hand.

'I won't be doing it,' I said. 'While this baby lives I'm going to give it every chance I can to survive.'

I pulled my trousers back up and stomped out the hospital.

A couple of weeks later I was back for another scan. Before I'd even laid on the bed the woman at the screen was giving me sympathetic smiles. She obviously thought my baby would already be dead. When she started scanning me again there were the same hesitant pauses and comings and goings around the monitor. Finally, I was let in on what was happening.

'Well, Mrs McKinley, something extraordinary seems to have happened,' the doctor said. 'The fibroid has not grown any more, in fact we think it may have shrunk slightly. It may be that the pregnancy has stopped it developing.'

'So the baby's going to be alright?' I said.

'Ah now, that brings me to my second point,' he went on. 'Although the fibroid appears to be reducing, we are concerned about other aspects of the foetus' development.'

In those few seconds I'd got my hopes up so high and now they were about to come smashing down again.

'We think the baby may have severe abnormalities. We'll need to scan you again in another fortnight to see what those are.'

Another two weeks went past. Another scan. Another load of bad news.

'We think your baby has some genetic condition which is preventing it from forming properly,' the doctor said. 'We think your child will be born severely disabled and the likelihood is that it will be deaf, dumb and blind. I appreciate this is difficult for you but we do suggest you again consider having a termination.'

'No,' I said. 'No way. I told you before, I'm going to do everything in my power to keep this baby alive – and nothing you say is going to change that.'

I was a devout Catholic and opposition to termination was part of my faith but my objections were based on more than that. Three of my babies had died because they hadn't been strong enough to fight for themselves. Now I had a baby who despite everything was clearly a fighter – I refused to be the one who stopped his chance for life. And of course there was the message that the nun had given me, that I would give birth to a healthy little boy. It was a straw, but I was clutching at it.

As the weeks passed the doctors' prognosis just got worse and worse. They said the foetus had fluid on the brain, only one leg and just one kidney.

'Your baby is going to be in pain from the moment it is born,' one doctor told me. 'Is that fair? We really do advise a termination.'

'And I advise you to stick your termination up your arse,' I replied. The more they went on at me about it, the more I was determined not to give in. I felt I was the only person in the world that my baby could count on to fight his corner. I couldn't let him down now.

Stevie was trying his hardest to do the right thing and hold down a job, but it didn't come natural to him. In the end he came up with his perfect solution for any kind of problem – running away!

'Let's go down and stay with my family in the West Country again,' he said. 'They're on a site near the sea and the kids would love it. Come on, it'll be a new start.'

I was sick of everything back in Manchester; Mammy, Daddy, the doctors, the rain! I hadn't been travelling for a few years by then and the thought of living in a trailer near a beach was certainly appealing. I'd take Danny and Pauly with us and the others could stay with Daddy or Bridget. And being a traveller, I knew if it really didn't work out in Cornwall, I could always come back. I did worry about the kids missing out at school and Sarah-Jane feeling uprooted but I knew that unlike my parents I'd make sure that the kids carried on with their education wherever we were living.

'OK,' I said. 'Let's do it.'

17

A Miracle

It was a ten-hour journey down to Cornwall with the six of us crammed into our beat-up old Vauxhall but finally we arrived at the site. The kids were hungry and shattered. I was feeling huge and uncomfortable with the baby. Stevie's cousin met us and showed us to the spare trailer he had for us at the side of the site.

Oh my God. What a pit.

'Is that it?' asked Stevie.

'Ay,' said his cousin. 'I said it was a bit rough and ready but it'll be grand once you get it fixed up.'

'Rough and ready?' I said. 'It's a complete dump!'

But we couldn't travel back the ten hours to Manchester and Stevie wanted to make a go of it – so that's what we did.

The caravan was about 12ft long and that was all the space we had for the four kids, him, me and my massive baby bump. It was filthy dirty and it smelt dank and damp. It must have been shut up for years. I was already sick with worry thinking about all the things that were going to be wrong with my baby and now I was living in a tiny trailer with rain pouring in the ceiling and damp lining the walls.

I made an appointment at the local hospital and soon I was back and forward for more scans and tests and investigations. The doctors confirmed everything that had been said in Manchester about how severely disabled the baby was.

One day a doctor sat me down in his office. 'Mrs McKinley, I have to prepare you for the worst. Within minutes of being born, your baby is going to die. He has no kidneys and won't be able to survive outside the womb. I'm so sorry to have to tell you this but you need to be aware so it isn't a terrible shock.'

'OK,' I said quietly. I was shattered after months of bleak diagnoses but I was still pleased I hadn't gone through with the termination. At least the baby would feel life, if only for a few breaths.

I went home so upset I couldn't even speak. Things were already fraught with Stevie again. He couldn't cope living all cooped up with the kids and surprise, surprise, the work he'd been promised had never materialised. He had no job, no money, no peace – well that's what he said – so he did what he always did and went out drinking.

I'd done my best to fix up the trailer. I'd bought some fabric in the market and sewn some curtains and I'd scrubbed the floor till you could just about see the pattern on the floor tiles again through years of ingrained filth. But it was still rank. There was just one bed, which me and Stevie shared with Pauly, Danny, Sarah-Jane and Tyrone. At least on the nights when Stevie didn't come home there was more room for the rest of us.

Pauly was nine and Sarah-Jane was six by then so I enrolled them at the local school while Danny and Tyrone stayed home with me during the days.

There was a two-ring gas hob in the trailer on which it was just about possible to cook a meal although that meant the whole place getting so steamed up that there would be small rivers running down the inside of the windows.

The whole place usually stank of leaking gas and I made sure we slept with the windows open rather than die from inhaling lethal fumes. But that meant at night we would be freezing. Even all cuddled up together under a pile of blankets we would still be shivering.

There was a hole in the seal of the roof, which leaked real bad every time it rained. If I thought it was going to be a wet night I'd get the plastic bucket out and line it up beneath where the leak was. But all night long we'd be hearing the plop, plop, plop of rainwater into the bucket.

All our clothes got damp hanging in the cupboard and one morning I took out Sarah-Jane's shoes and found they were covered in mildew. The kids were only little and I was heavily pregnant but we were living in a health hazard.

Stevie's cousins lived on a house at the edge of the site and sometimes they'd take pity on me and let us cook our food there. But the rest of the time we were stuck together in the trailer.

'We can't stay here,' I complained to Stevie one night. 'I want to go home.'

'You want to go running back to your family as normal I suppose,' he said. 'Well, we're staying here with my people for a while whether you like it or not.'

So we stayed.

I was seven months pregnant that Christmas and was feeling dreadful. On a regular check-up at the doctor I told him how bad I'd been. He did a few tests and diagnosed pneumonia. The GP asked where I was living and what the conditions were like. Bit by bit I told him about the leaking roof and the mildew on the walls.

'I'm admitting you to hospital,' he said.

I can't go,' I replied. 'What about the kids?'

'I'm sure you've got other family members who can help out the week before Christmas,' he said. 'And seeing as how you are insistent on going through with this pregnancy you need to be in the best physical condition to cope with it.'

Stevie's cousin agreed to look after the kids and I went into hospital. Just being somewhere dry and warm felt like moving to a palace. And I knew the kids were in the warmth of a house too so I didn't feel so guilty about leaving them.

But on Christmas Eve I couldn't stay away any longer. When I was a little girl Christmas had always been a really big event in our family and I'd always made sure it was the same for my kids too. I'd already bought their toys and hidden them round Stevie's cousin's house but I still needed to wrap them, put up a tree and some decorations in the trailer, leave out all Santa's bits, get the food shopping in and start preparing a turkey.

'I'm discharging myself,' I told the nurse on duty.

'I don't think you should be doing that,' she replied. 'Why?'

'Because I've got a lorry load of presents to wrap and a turkey dinner to cook on a two-ring hob!' I replied.

When I got back to the site I asked if I could cook our turkey in the cousin's kitchen and popped it in her oven. We hadn't been invited in there for our lunch even though loads of other relatives were going round. I tried not to be hurt and got on with preparing the rest of the veg and potatoes on our two rings as best as I could.

Then I rang Stevie and asked him to pick up the kids' presents. As main presents I'd got Sarah-Jane a Barbie scooter that she'd been asking for for months, a new bike for Pauly and an Action Man for Danny and Tyrone. All Stevie had to do was collect them, wrap them, then leave them in the boot of the car until the kids went to sleep.

In the meantime I boiled a ham, then when it was cooked I covered it in tin foil and left it on the only bit of counter space that there was in the tiny trailer. No sooner had I done that than it started to rain and water started dripping, splosh, splosh, splosh, straight on to the tin foil. But I just had to leave it; there was not a single other scrap of space in the place.

Then I bathed the kids in the tin bath in the middle of the trailer floor and tied up Sarah-Jane's hair in rags to make it beautiful and curly for Christmas morning.

When the kids were finally asleep in bed I was up and down outside the trailer making Santa footprints in the mud with flour. Then I came back in and started preparing the vegetables.

After I'd done all that I went up to the cousin's house where everyone else in the family was now well into the party spirit. But when I looked in the oven there was my turkey all dried out and totally useless. There had been a houseful of women up there but not one of them had checked whether my turkey was OK. I lifted it out of the oven and threw it straight in the bin.

Christmas was already a disaster but at least I'd got all the presents sorted in advance. But when I looked out the window, Stevie's car with the kids' presents in the boot, was missing.

'Oh God no,' I thought. 'Whatever else, Santa has to come on Christmas morning.'

I walked back up to the cousin's house, borrowed a car then spent two hours driving from pub to pub looking for Stevie.

It was gone midnight when I finally tracked him down and rescued the presents, brought them home and left them in a big pile in the living room of the trailer.

Finally I fell into bed about half three in the morning. I was exhausted. Half an hour later Stevie came in so drunk he could hardly walk or talk. I couldn't sleep for the smell of beer coming off him. Then he started farting. There was all six of us in the bed but he was spreadeagled in the middle. I ended up sitting scrunched up in the corner, my face pressed up against the condensation on the window and listening to Stevie snoring and the rainwater dripping on my ham.

The next morning the kids couldn't even put on their new Christmas clothes because Stevie had fallen asleep on them and couldn't be woken. They stood outside in their pyjamas in the pouring rain, Sarah-Jane's curls getting soaked.

'Daddy will be up soon and then we can unwrap the presents,' I said, attempting to sound jolly. When Stevie did finally crawl out of his pit in the middle of the morning the kids were beside themselves with excitement.

Sarah-Jane started ripping the paper off her present as I stirred some bread sauce on the hob. I heard her wail and turned round to see her holding an Action Man.

'Mammy, why has Santa sent me this?' she cried. 'He must think I'm a really naughty girl because he knows I don't like Action Man. Do you think Santa hates me?'

Tyrone was looking equally confused by his pink Barbie Scooter with flashing handlebars.

I glared at Stevie. The only thing he'd had to do was wrap and label the presents and he hadn't even managed that!

I looked at the ham, which by then was soaked in brown coloured rainwater. I couldn't give that to the kids. I lobbed that in the bin too. For Christmas lunch we had cheese sandwiches.

'Happy Christmas, kids,' I said, trying to raise a smile. Stevie went to the pub.

That whole time in the trailer was a grim period. The only thing that kept me going was thinking that so long as the little baby inside me kept fighting, I had to do the same.

As it got closer and closer to my due date I became more and more terrified. I could feel the baby kicking inside me. When Sarah-Jane and Tyrone were running around the trailer screaming and laughing, he'd kick even faster. I truly believed he wanted to be out there playing with his brother and sister. But that was never going to happen. The doctors had all assured me that he wouldn't even make it home from hospital to meet them.

At night I'd lay in bed rubbing my bump and talking to the baby. I felt this was our only chance to be together. It was so strange because as he was approaching life, he was approaching death too. I cried and cried night and day. It was so unfair. I'd been given this baby growing inside me and now it was going to be taken away before I even had a chance to get to know him.

At 38 weeks the doctors decided to induce labour. They thought that the earlier the child was born the safer it would be for me. They were adamant there was no hope for the baby.

Bridget had come down to be with me for the birth while Stevie stayed in the trailer to look after the kids. Labour was awful because I knew when it was over, things were most likely only going to get worse. But Bridget mopped my forehead and kept me calm as the pains came quicker and stronger. When the time came for me to push, the delivery room was total chaos. There were three paediatricians waiting for the baby to come plus a midwife, two nurses, Bridget and me.

Finally the little mite burst out. Despite all the people in the room there was total silence. The midwife cut the umbilical cord and one of the paediatricians picked up the baby and dashed straight out the door with him.

I was left there panting and exhausted and without the baby I'd carried for the past nine months.

'What the hell's going on?' I said. 'Tell me. What's going on?'

'The doctors are just examining him,' the midwife said.

'But is he alive?' I asked. 'I just want to hold him in my arms, whatever he is.'

A couple of minutes later the doctor reappeared holding the baby wrapped in a white cotton blanket. He handed him to me and I held him right close. He had a perfect pink face, tiny screwed-up eyes and ten beautiful fingers sticking out the blanket. And he was alive. I knew instinctively he was alive.

'He's OK,' I said, stunned.

At that moment the baby broke out into the loudest, healthiest cry I'd ever heard.

'He's not just OK,' said the paediatrician. 'He's a bloody miracle!'

Me and Bridget were laughing and crying then crying and laughing. We couldn't believe it. The nun had been right all along, I'd got my healthy boy. I called him Finn.

His feet were both badly squashed backwards and would need surgery to correct them but they were both there, unlike what I'd been told. And there was no question that he was deaf, blind or dumb. As for his kidneys, they were quite small but they were working.

As a precaution, Finn was taken to the intensive care unit. Two hours later the four paediatricians were standing over his incubator. They were concerned that he still hadn't passed urine and feared there may be greater problems with his kidneys.

Then all of a sudden, like the spray from a garden hose, Finn pissed over the lot of them. He really was my miracle. And he still is.

18

Trailer Life by the Sea

Some days I'd just sit in the chair and stare at Finn. I really couldn't believe he was there.

His brother and sister adored him and even when he was tiny he would watch them intently from his cot, just as I'd been sure he wanted to join in their games when he was still in my belly. So many times I'd think that if I'd listened to the doctors' advice he would have been terminated before birth and he would never ever have existed. I thanked God for giving him to me.

Finn was a bright ray of sunshine in an otherwise difficult time. As well as surgery on his feet to bend them back into the correct position Finn needed intensive physiotheraphy, which meant weekly 60-mile round journeys to the nearest hospital with the other kids in the back of the car every time. Of course Stevie was nowhere to be seen on those days.

Conditions in the trailer were only getting worse. The leaks seemed to be contagious because before long, on wet days I had three buckets and two saucepans on the floor catching the drips. The sheets and blankets on the bed felt constantly damp and the kids went from one cough and cold straight into the next. I had two chest infections and it was no good for the baby's health either. I decided we had to get out, whatever Stevie thought. He was hardly ever there anyway.

My doctor had suggested to me that we should consider moving to a hostel in Exeter. We'd be nearer the hospital for Finn's physiotherapy treatment and most importantly, it would be warm and dry. Stevie hadn't been around for a few days so I left a message with his cousin that we were off, packed our belongings into the old Vauxhall Nova and left that stinking hell hole for the last time.

We all shared one big room in the hostel but we each had our own bed and there was a big cot for Finn. After where we'd come from, it felt like luxury. The people that ran the hostel were really kind and I felt safe there. We didn't hear a whisper from Stevie, which was, frankly, a relief. After six months the council managed to find us a house. There had been squatters in there before us and when I opened the door, I saw the house was in a terrible condition. The walls were filthy, there were awful stains on the carpets and I even found used syringes upstairs. But the council helped me clear it all out and in a few weeks we'd got it all fixed up really nice. I spent ages choosing the right colour to paint the walls and selecting my curtain fabric. When I was finished it looked like a palace.

This was going to be our new beginning. I was dead proud.

And then Stevie turned up again. Each time he came back to me he seemed a little more pitiful and I felt a bit more sorry for him. He was getting older and years of drinking and partying hadn't been kind to him. He was looking tired and his hands shook terribly. Despite everything that had happened between us, I still had a soft spot for him. We'd known each other since we were kids and if he begged me to come back, I didn't have the heart to say no to him. But something had changed between us.

I'd grown up a lot and getting my own council house at
the other end of the country to my family had made me
realise I was quite capable of standing on my own two
feet. I was feeling stranger then I had done for years and
for the first time I felt divorce was an option for me. Yes,
I might be ostracised but maybe I had to rist that for the
sake of my kids. From now on our marriage was going to
be on my terms. So when Stevie started drinking again
after a couple of weeks back home I told him to sling his
hook. I wasn't going to have that kind of behaviour
around the kids. He'd never laid a finger on me again
after the night of the very bad beating in Manchester.
Now when I told him to clear off he just quietly packed
his bags and went.

A couple of days after he left I decided I needed to go on
the Pill – just so I was prepared for the next time he turned
up and talked me into bed. I went to the doctor's and got
the prescription. I had to take the first pill as soon as my
next period ended.

Except my next period never came. Yes, I was pregnant
again. He'd only been back a fortnight and we'd only slept
together a couple of times. I couldn't believe it was happening. I loved all my children but I was bringing them up
single handed, looking after Danny with all his special
needs, and taking Finn for physio several times a week. I
had no idea how I'd cope with another baby.

But if it was God's will I decided that what would be
would be.

Except this time, I wasn't putting myself through all
the terrifying conversations with doctors, midwives and
health visitors. They'd given me nothing but stress last

time. And they'd almost convinced me to abort my beloved baby boy, Finn. So the first time I saw a doctor during the entire pregnancy was a week before what I'd worked out to be my due date.

When I went to the hospital and was taken to see a doctor, he couldn't believe it.

'Are you mad?' he said. 'You've got to 39 weeks pregnant and you've had no scans, no blood or urine tests, no blood pressure taken, no examinations. What were you thinking of?'

But I wasn't taking any more bullying from doctors. 'I was thinking about my baby,' I said. 'Last time I was pregnant it seemed to me that every doctor I came across was telling me to get rid of him and he is now in great health. So this time I decided to go it alone.'

I even shocked myself with my forcefulness. But I was changing. I was growing up. I'd always known my own mind but more and more I wasn't afraid to voice it. Doctors and teachers and country people generally didn't scare me so much as they once had. I might not have their education and their accents but inside we were all just the same.

'OK,' said the doctor. 'Well you're here now. I suppose we had better get you checked out.'

Three days later, on October 3 1996, I gave birth naturally to another gorgeous little girl who I named Grace.

Stevie came round to see the baby but that time when he turned up he looked in an even worse state than ususal. He'd always been quite handsome but he looked exhausted and what had once been laughter lines on his face were now deep wrinkles.

He'd been drinking increasingly heavily over the past couple of years and hanging around with a bad crowd who were into drugs and all sorts. It suited me that when he was with that gang he kept as far away from me and the kids as possible. He didn't stop long before disappearing again.

Soon after Grace's birth I started suffering terrible pains in my stomach. The doctors detected a problem with my ovaries, which needed surgery. Stevie's family offered to look after the kids and I went back into hospital again. I'd just been wheeled back on to the ward and was coming round from the surgery when the nurse brought the ward telephone to me. It was Sarah-Jane, who by then was eight years old.

'Oh Mammy,' she said. 'Daddy came round last night and he gave the keys for your car to his mates. They went out driving in it but they were blind drunk and they've smashed it up. It's all burnt out and it's there on the front drive now like a piece of scrap.'

I was still groggy from the anaesthetic and it took a while to take in what she was saying. But when I did, I was raging. How would I get Finn to his physio appointments now? That was my car, but as with everything, Stevie had gone and ruined it.

I put the phone down, trying not to worry too much and closed my eyes again. But just five minutes later the nurse was back with the phone. This time it was a nurse calling from a psychiatric unit. The kids must have given her the ward number as the best way of contacting me.

'Mrs McKinley, your husband was admitted here last night. He is really not very well. Could you bring him some pyjamas and a toothbrush?'

I could barely move off the bed myself but a couple of hours later I struggled home, got Stevie's things and took them to the unit. He'd ended up there after police had picked him up. He'd taken his friends back to my house while I'd been in hospital and had a party. But when the booze ran out, a load of them had driven into town looking for more. It was then that they'd crashed the car. Maybe it was a cover-up or maybe he was seriously feeling sick, because Stevie had admitted himself to the psychiatric unit, saying he didn't think he could cope with life any more.

The following day, I was at home recovering from my operation, when his mother came to visit me. 'Please Rosie, take him back. He is in real trouble with his drinking and you know you're the only one he really respects.'

I wanted to help, I truly did. But his mother was wrong. Stevie wouldn't listen to me any more than he would listen to anyone else. And I knew from bitter experience that if someone has an addiction the only way they will get over it is if they themselves truly want to beat it.

'There's nothing I can do,' I told Stevie's mother. 'He's got to make the decision to help himself.'

'You're his wife,' she shouted. 'It's your duty to help get him better.'

Ah yes, 'a wife for life'. It was the same old thing all over again. Men could do whatever with whomever for as long as they wanted but when things started to go wrong it was the wife who was supposed to pick up the pieces. But with a new-born baby and Finn still needing regular treatment, Danny with all his problems plus the other two at school, I already had a fair bit on my plate to contend with.

'I'm sorry,' I said. 'If he comes back here I'll cook for him and look after him but I can't go out there begging him to live with me and to stay off the booze for ever. It just won't work.'

I might have sounded harsh, but I was thinking of

everything that had happened with Mammy. I'd worried myself sick about her in the early years of her alcoholism and it hadn't made the slightest bit of difference. Now I'd learnt that I should focus my efforts on the things I could change, like making sure the kids got a good education and Finn got all the medical treatment that he needed. I still spoke to Mammy on the telephone occasionally but she was rarely at home when I called.

I rang Daddy once or twice a week as well. If Shirley answered I'd just ask to be handed over to him. I can see now that what happened wasn't all Shirley's fault but I still found it hard to speak to her. The pain was just too raw. Daddy would sometimes tell me that he'd seen Mammy around the city. Usually she was lying on a park bench or outside one of the hostels for homeless people. She was drinking cider and super-strength lagers by then, anything that would get her drunk quickly and cheaply. Her hair was long and greasy and her clothes torn and stained. Countless numbers of people had tried to help her countless numbers of times. But I had realised that Mammy didn't want to help herself. And I feared that was the problem with Stevie too.

The next time I heard from Stevie he was on my front doorstep, so drunk that he'd thrown up all over my newly painted letterbox. I was furious.

'Take me back Rosie,' he begged. 'If you don't let me back in I'm going to kill myself.'

'No you will not,' I said. 'Now leave us alone.' It was a horrible card to play because however much I bluffed it out, I was left with this nagging thought that maybe one day he might actually hurt himself and it would be all my fault. So now he was torturing me mentally.

I managed to remain strong but his drunken suicide threats became more and more frequent. If I saw him lurching up the garden path I'd quickly pop on a DVD to keep the kids occupied in the hope they wouldn't notice what was going on. It was far too distressing for them to have to witness.

Then he started to break into the house when me and the kids weren't there. He would put his hand through the back door window and open the catch on the door from there. He'd let himself in, make a big fry-up then sit himself in the armchair in front of the telly. One evening I was bringing the kids back from the cinema when I saw the back window smashed again.

'Get out,' I said, seeing him slouched on the sofa.

'Won't,' came his reply.

'This is my house and I'm telling you to get out,' I said.

'And you're my wife, which makes this my house too,' he replied.

Normally I'd just leave him there and go to bed myself hoping that by the next morning he'd be gone, in search of another drink.

It was strange because for years Stevie had treated me like dirt. He hadn't shown the slightest interest in me and months could go by without even a phone call. But suddenly he was obsessed with me and couldn't keep away. Maybe he could sense I was becoming more independent and he was desperately trying to keep control of me.

One night I woke at about 3.30 in the morning and heard someone breathing in my bedroom. I could feel my stomach flipping with fear as I leant across to switch on the lamp. But when the light flicked on I couldn't believe my eyes – it was horrific. Stevie was there, totally covered in blood. There was blood all over his arms, clothes and trousers and it was dripping great spots onto my carpet. 'Are you happy now?' he growled. 'Are ya?'

He went into the bathroom and locked the door. I was terrified he was dying so I ran downstairs to call an ambulance. When I got to the hallway, I stopped in shock. There was blood splattered up both sides of the wall and even on the ceiling. My oak wood floor was scarlet and when I went into the kitchen there were huge great puddles on the floor tiles, which had splashed up the sides of the work units.

Stevie came down the stairs behind me and kicked the phone off the wall. He was raging and looked like something out of a horror film. I was terrified.

I ran out into the street and banged on my neighbour's door. 'Quick, please can you get me an ambulance,' I said.

When I went back to the house he was sitting on a sofa. Blood was still dripping from him although I still couldn't work out where the wound was. 'What have you done to yourself?' I kept asking, but he just couldn't answer me for groaning.

The paramedics said he'd cut the main artery in his hand. He must have done it while trying to climb in the back window of the house. His hand was sewn back together but I never did get the stains off my kitchen floor. By then I was on first-name terms with the glazier who kept coming out to repair the back window. I'd had enough. I was never going to get any peace in that house so I decided to move on somewhere that Stevie wouldn't be able to find us. I didn't care anymore if that wasn't what traveller women were supposed to do – it was what I wanted to do for me and for my children.

19

A New Beginning

We moved again to a house in the countryside near Plymouth. I liked that area of the country and felt it was far enough away from Exeter for Stevie not to be able to find me and the kids. I hated the children not seeing their Daddy but it seemed the fairest thing to do. It was upsetting for them having to watch him turn up and start ranting and raving.

We rented a bright flat with enough room for the lot of us, and the kids settled into their new school. This hadn't been what I'd wanted for my children, that they should move from pillar to post, constantly having their education disrupted and having to make new friends. I'd wanted them to have stability but it wasn't working out that way after all. I felt guilty about that but I also had to keep us all clear of Stevie's increasingly strange behaviour.

We settled in well. I had a distant cousin, Trisha, living nearby and she showed us around. I even went out for a drink with her sometimes in the evening. I felt like an independent woman for the first time and that was good. I'd had quite enough of men. I really had no interest in them at all. Even if a man tried to chat me up in the pub, I'd just walk away. It didn't even cross my mind to get involved with anyone. Despite everything I still had a husband and I wouldn't be unfaithful to him. I also knew that through his traveller connections, Stevie probably had a good idea where

I was but was choosing to leave us alone. But if I ever got involved with another man I'd never have a second's peace.

Sometimes, when the kids were in bed and I was sat in front of the telly on my own again, I did feel very lonely but I couldn't face the aggro of another relationship. And with the kids to look after and a home to keep up there was no time for any of that business anyway.

I decided to use my time in the evenings more constructively. One evening I was sat on the sofa and started flicking through Tyrone's schoolbooks. He was still only six but I struggled to read many of the words he'd tried to write in his big, round handwriting and I felt deeply ashamed. It had been years since I'd last thought of it but suddenly I was hit by the desire to learn again. From then on I'd sit with Tyrone and Sarah-Jane's books every night, trying to remind myself of the different sounds of the letters and merging them to make words, the way my teacher had showed me years earlier. It was hard work but I was determined to do it.

Each time I finished one of those books meant for a primary-school child I'd get a rush of satisfaction. It was slow progress, but I was getting there.

And then Stevie turned up again. He said he'd known where we were for ages but wanted to get himself together before coming to see us. He certainly seemed a lot more sorted. He looked fuller in the face, he was off the booze and he was driving a smart car.

'You can stay for the weekend,' I said cautiously.

By the Monday morning he'd found himself some work and hadn't gone near a drink. I let him stay some more. The kids were completely delighted to have him around.

We were together then for a year – it was the longest we'd ever managed in more than ten years of marriage. He really had changed and stayed off the drink and held down a job. The only problem was that he didn't like the way that I'd also changed and become more independent. Every time I left the house he'd quiz me on where I was going or who I was with. All those years when he'd disappeared for month after month without a word of explanation and now I wasn't allowed to go across the street without telling him my precise movements. He didn't like me practising my reading either. Maybe he thought getting an education would take me even further away from him. He was constantly trying to control me and I found that very hard but while he was sober I allowed him to stay, for the sake of the children and the family life that we seemed, finally, to have.

But then, after a year of relative peace, he fell off the wagon. He started drinking again, worse than ever. There was nothing concrete that triggered the relapse but when you're an alcoholic, the risk is always there. Maybe it was because he'd stayed off it for so long that when he fell it was really bad, but whatever the reasons, he was drinking morning, noon and night. I kicked him out of the house immediately, but then life became a nightmare with him turning up at all times of the day and night, demanding to be let in.

One day I popped out to the shop at the end of our road. Pauly was 13 by then so I left him and Sarah-Jane with instructions to keep an eye on the others and said I'd be back in ten minutes.

I was only in the shop long enough to buy some bread

and ham for lunch but when I walked back down the road
I could see my car was missing from out the front of the
house. Surely it hadn't been nicked. When I got to the door,
Sarah-Jane was looking terrified. 'I'm sorry Mammy but
Daddy came round and said he needed to borrow your car.
And he took Finn with him.'

For a moment it felt like my heart was stopping. 'Had he
been drinking?'

'I'm not sure,' Sarah-Jane said. 'His breath did smell
funny.'

Oh God. The thought of Stevie drink-driving with Finn
in the back of the car made me feel sick. And knowing
Stevie, they could be gone for weeks. Finn still needed
intense therapy at least twice a day and there was no way
Stevie would be doing that.

I rang the police and anyone who might have any idea
where Stevie had gone. Nothing.

For a week I barely ate or slept. My miracle boy had
never spent a night away from me before and it was
breaking my heart. I walked for miles on the off chance
I might see the car parked up somewhere, but there was
no sign of it.

Finally I got a call from one of Stevie's cousins telling me
the name of a pub where he was at that very moment,
drinking with pals. But it was 60 miles away! I borrowed a
car from my neighbour, loaded the other kids in the back
and drove as fast as I could to the pub he had told me about.
Then I parked up nearby and crept down to the pub and
looked in the window. Stevie was in there with a load of his
old pals from that town but Finn was nowhere to be seen. I
realised he must have left him with one of his mates' wives

so I drove around the town, desperately trying to remember whereabouts they had all lived. After almost two hours I drove along a shabby little road on the edge of an estate and saw Finn on the verge, playing on his own. His hands and face were black with dirt and he was still wearing the clothes he'd had on the morning he'd disappeared.

I jumped out of the car and wrapped my arms around him, almost sobbing with relief. The other kids were right behind me and were hugging and kissing him too. But I was terrified the woman in the house was about to come out and see us and would be straight on the phone to Stevie in the pub.

'Come on, Finn,' I said. 'Let's get home.'

'Oh no Mammy,' he said. 'I've got to stay here with Daddy. He'll be back soon and he said if I went off with you I'd never see him again. Sorry, Mammy.' Finn was still only four and was the sweetest child; he'd have hated to do something that his Daddy had told him was wrong.

I was terrified Stevie would be back from the pub raging drunk at any moment and he'd go mad if he saw me there. 'Please love,' I said. 'Of course you'll see Daddy again, but I just need you to come with me now.'

'Oh, I don't think I should Mammy. I don't want to upset Daddy,' little Finn replied.

Finally, with a lot of promises about bags of chips on the way home, he agreed to come with us.

I'd only got around the corner when the front offside tyre went flat – I must have had a slow puncture. Could this day get any more stressful? But I wasn't stopping for anything so close to where Stevie might be. I drove the car along on a flat tyre for ten miles before I felt safe enough to get out and change it. I didn't care what damage I did to the wheel, we needed to get away.

We spent the next week staying in bed and breakfasts until finally I felt it was safe enough to go home.

But still Stevie didn't give up. One morning in the middle of the school summer holidays he turned up blind drunk. 'I want to see me kids,' he shouted, banging at the front door.

'No, sorry,' I replied, my hands trembling. 'You can't see them when you're drunk. Come back when you're sober.'

I locked all the windows, closed the curtains and turned the telly up loud. But I could still hear him going mad outside. 'Open the fucking door,' he was yelling.

'What's Daddy saying?' said Sarah-Jane.

'He's saying he's going to kill you Mammy,' chipped in Tyrone. 'Why's he saying that Mammy?'

I was terrified and called the police, who turned up and talked him into leaving.

The next day he was back again but this time it was with a knife in his hand. That time he was there for an hour and a half before the police turned up and took him away.

It was a boiling hot summer but I was too frightened to leave the house to even go to the corner shop. And I made the kids stay inside all the time, which was driving us all mad.

'This fella's never going to give up,' one of the police officers told me. 'I probably shouldn't say this, but if I was you, I'd move.'

It broke my heart to leave the house that I'd worked so hard to make a home but I knew it was the only way to really be rid of Stevie once and for all. His relapse back into drinking and especially his kidnapping of Finn had shown me that nothing was ever going to change and that

Stevie couldn't be any kind of father. I had long ago stopped thinking he could be a husband, and now as far as I was concerned, he had blown every chance going. We just needed to be somewhere safe, and I knew that all the restraining orders in the world wouldn't keep him away from me if I stayed put.

So we were on the move again.

I didn't mind going somewhere where I didn't know a soul in the world. All I wanted was a little bit of peace. I piled the kids into the car and drove towards Bristol. I wanted to stay in the south-west of England but I felt it was a city big enough for us to get lost in. No one would know us and no one would be sticking their nose into our business.

In Bristol we were back to sharing a room in a hostel but this time, it was grim. I couldn't even have a bath without taking all the kids with me because you weren't allowed to leave them alone for a moment. There were people constantly coming and going and we had money nicked, clothes nicked, toys nicked. Even margarine out the fridge was taken!

After that we stayed in a few temporary flats but they weren't much better. The first I hated because there were drug deals going on along the corridor and the second was just as rough, with the youngsters prowling round the estate in gangs. There was no way I wanted my kids growing up in a place like this.

We went on the waiting list for a council house but in the meantime I felt the safest place for us to be would be back in a trailer, so I found out about a site near the city centre and scraped together enough money to rent a trailer for a while from someone living there. I was careful not to give away too much information about us to anyone on the site.

I mixed with the people there but made sure I never gave away anything that could get back to Stevie.

For more than a year I didn't ring or see anyone in my family apart from two phone calls to Bridget. I didn't want anyone to know where I was and I was well aware that if I told just one person, the news would spread like wildfire around the traveller grapevine.

'Are y'alright Rosie?' Bridget would say when I called her.

'Yes, B,' I'd say. 'We're all fine. But please, please don't ask me where we are or I'll never be able to call you again. I'm so sorry but I just can't tell anyone. I trust you completely but if someone got the truth out of you about where we are, my life wouldn't be worth living. Listen, tell me how yous are. Are Mammy and Daddy OK?'

I even found myself a job – the first I'd had since I worked as a trainee chef as a teenager. My new job was helping to care for the elderly in an old folks' home. I loved it there and I think I was pretty good at it too. I'd wash and look after the residents and stop for a chat on my way around the home. It made me feel independent and I liked that. I wasn't dependent on anyone else for money and I had something in my life that was just for me. In the evenings I went back to trying to teach myself to read using the kids' schoolbooks.

Then one day, a man who managed the site where we were living told me about an education group for travellers. It met once a week and helped people from the travelling community with reading, writing and simple arithmetic. At first I just dismissed the idea. I didn't want to advertise to the world that I struggled with reading and understanding, I'd rather get on with my learning on my own.

For weeks I chewed the idea over in my mind before resolving I'd go along once, just to see what it was like. There was certainly plenty I still needed to learn. I'd been to eight different schools as a kid but here I was in my thirties and still only able to read the simplest words. I could just about read a menu in a café but as soon as it was a word like 'broccoli' or 'pineapple' I'd be totally stumped. If we were driving anywhere I'd have to get the kids to help me with complicated road signs and if any official letters came about our child benefit or my tax credits, I would spend hours deciphering them, letter by letter.

I also struggled with knowing what a lot of words meant. People would be talking about things and I wouldn't have a clue what they were on about. I suppose Mammy and Daddy had always used quite simple language and I'd inherited that from them. There had been thousands of times when I was growing up when I'd stand there red-faced and mortified because I couldn't pronounce a word or because someone was asking me a question and I really couldn't understand what they were trying to find out.

The classes were held in a community centre and about 20 travellers of all ages sat around at desks. Some of them I recognised from our site but others were total strangers. Like me, none of them had had much of an education, moving from school to school with very little time to learn much along the way.

I loved that first class though. I wasn't made to feel stupid for a moment and I left at the end of the evening with a real thrill from having learnt something new.

My teacher was a young woman with long, curly, red hair called Sally. She was a bit of a hippie and was still wearing tie-dye skirts years after they'd gone out of fashion. The travellers in the group were of massively differing abilities but she made sure she spent time with everyone there, talking to them and encouraging them. She spent ages helping me.

'You're going to be great at this,' she said to me that first evening.

'Yeah, right!' I joked. But inside I wondered if she might be right. For the first time, someone was showing faith in me and that gave me an immediate burst of confidence.

'But there are so many words,' I said. 'And I feel so stupid when people are talking and I don't understand them.'

'Well, your reading is coming along so if there is a word you don't understand just look it up in a dictionary and it'll give you the meaning,' she said.

Why hadn't I ever thought of that?

The next morning I was straight into WHSmith's to buy a dictionary and I spent the rest of the day poring over all those words that had terrified me for so many years. Things like 'psychology', 'intimidate', 'approximation'. They are words that most people might grow up using and understanding but as a kid I'd never heard them and they'd never become part of my vocabulary.

I loved those classes and at the end of each one I'd go home with armfuls of work books to practise my comprehension and sentence construction. With the help of my new dictionary I was also reading more and more at home. It'd be anything I could get my hands on: library books, newspapers, magazines. Reading made me feel part of the wider world. I wasn't just stranded in the travelling community any more. Of course I was still part of it but I finally felt I belonged to something bigger too, where I could be whatever I wanted to be.

I made rapid progress in my learning and soon I was helping Sally teach the travellers who were still struggling with the simpler words. I was useful to her too because often when she said a word in her Angela Rippon accent the travellers would all stare at her in total bewilderment. But when I repeated the word in my familiar traveller voice, everyone in the room would get their heads down and start trying to write it.

Teaching others how to sound out the words and complete a sentence gave me a massive buzz. I was showing that I could actually be good at something other than cleaning and caring for other people. And I was helping members of my community too. I decided then that this was going to be my future.

Sally encouraged me to enrol in another night class for all sorts of people with literacy problems. Again I was reluctant to go at first. It was one thing exposing my ignorance in front of a group of travellers but it was quite another doing it in front of country people.

'I won't go,' I told Sally. 'They'll laugh at me.'

'No they won't,' she said. 'They will all be in the same situation as you.'

'Look, you weren't laughed at by settled people at every school you ever went to, were you? But I was and so I won't be going.'

The conversation went on like that for quite a while until Sally offered to come with me for the first session. I was touched that she was being so generous with her time. Grudgingly, I agreed.

When I got there I was amazed. There was a roomful of people and most of them couldn't read or write as well as me. No one laughed or sniggered at anyone. In fact, it was an incredible atmosphere. Everyone was so supportive of each other because we were all there for the same reason, to get the education that, for whatever reason, we'd missed out on as kids.

We learned more advanced grammar: verbs, adverbs, adjectives and nouns. The way sentences were put together began to make sense and reading became easier and easier. From then on I'd go to the travellers' class every Tuesday night and the settled people's class on a Thursday. I'd got the learning bug and next I decided I wanted to learn computing.

I enrolled in another class and learnt keyboard skills, basic word-processing skills and how to use the internet. My world was getting broader and broader and I loved it. I saved up my wages from the care home and bought a computer. Soon I was on it every night, emailing friends from all over the country and reading anything and everything.

And I loved being able to help the kids with their home-work. When Sarah-Jane had been very little I'd struggled with my words but now I could help both her and Tyrone with their English and maths in the evenings. I could see they were impressed by their mum and that felt good.

But some of my traveller friends on the site were suspicious of all my learning and classes. 'You're becoming a right country girl,' one of my mates said one evening when I told her I couldn't go for a drink because I had an extra evening class.

'I am not,' I said. 'I'm a traveller, I always will be. All I'm doing is getting an education – you should try it!'

Finally, after two years of waiting we reached the top of the council list and got our own three-bedroom house. It was a big house in a nice area. There was a garden for the kids and after a bit of work I made it clean and bright. I was determined this was the place we were going to stay. I was exhausted from moving and felt ready to settle down. I just wanted a bit of peace to enjoy my children, give them a stable life and work on my education. Oh, I loved the peace in that house. I hadn't heard a word from Stevie in all that time and I really did feel free of him.

Life was good. Or so I thought.

20

Wedding Bells

It was Sarah-Jane's sixteenth birthday and she was so excited about her big day. I gave her some money to go into town with some friends to do a bit of shopping and to treat themselves to a pizza on the way home. They were just waiting for a bus to come home when Sarah-Jane turned around and there in front of her was Stevie. He was drunk and lurching along the pavement.

'Hey, it's my little girl all grown up. Don't you want to come and give your Daddy a hug?'

Sarah-Jane was mortified that all her friends were watching what was going on. She had always adored her father but this was so embarrassing for a teenage girl. She'd told her friends that her parents were separated but hadn't admitted that the reason she didn't have contact with her father was because he was an alcoholic.

'Hello Daddy,' Sarah-Jane said quietly.

'Here love, take this,' he said and he handed her a bundle of notes.

When Sarah-Jane got home she was quiet and obviously upset. 'Didn't you have a good time, love?' I asked.

'I saw my daddy,' she said and I felt my blood run cold. Here we go again, I thought. 'Why can't he just be like the other girls' daddy's?' she asked.

I had no answer for that. All I could do was give her a

hug. We put the cash away in a pot in the kitchen that Sarah-Jane was using to save up for her own computer and I tried not to panic, but I was terrified at the thought that Stevie had tracked us down after all those years of being free from him.

A fortnight later I nipped out to buy a loaf of bread from the local shop. I'd parked the car outside the shop and had just got back into it and was doing up my seatbelt when I saw a jeep speeding towards me on the wrong side of the road. It was coming full pelt and at that moment I was convinced I was about to die. It was too late to get out of the car so I just sat there and waited for the collision. At the very last second the driver slammed on his brakes and the jeep screeched to a standstill just a couple of millimetres from the front of my car.

I looked up and saw Stevie in the driving seat.

He had a murderous look on his face and even though I hadn't seen him for more than three years I knew instantly he'd been drinking.

'What did you do with my cash?' he yelled as he jumped out of the jeep. He was in a ripping temper. 'What did you do with it?' he said, grabbing my arm.

I could feel myself starting to shake all over again. 'What are you talking about?' I said.

'I found Sarah-Jane and said I needed my money back,' he yelled. 'She told me you'd put it in a pot in the kitchen. Thieving off your own daughter, you should be ashamed.' Then he suddenly smacked me around the face. It was years since he'd done that but it brought back all the feelings of shame and misery I'd lived with for years.

I didn't react to the smack, even though my face was

stinging like fury. And I couldn't be bothered to explain about Sarah-Jane saving for a computer or how upset she had been to see him again. I couldn't be bothered with any of it. I reached down inside the car and took three £20 notes out of my purse. I handed them to him and got back into the driving seat.

For a while he paced up and down outside my car. I was totally blocked in by his jeep in front and another car behind me, but eventually he roared off and, trembling, I drove home.

I couldn't understand how he'd found us again after I'd tried so hard to keep our new home secret. I never did find out but I'd learnt by then it was impossible to keep anything quiet in the traveller community. The kids all had friends from traveller families and I suppose one of them must have passed on the word to him.

I reported what had happened to the police and they fitted a panic button in the house so I'd get an immediate response if he turned up again drunk or violent. That made me feel a lot calmer about things. I was determined not to lose another home. I had made a vow not to let Stevie's problems ruin the life I was building for myself and the kids, and I wasn't going to break it.

By then Sarah-Jane had got herself a boyfriend, Jason, who was from a travelling family. They'd met at a disco and he was a nice boy from a good family in Ireland who'd been living on a site in Bristol for a couple of years.

I'd brought up Sarah-Jane to know right from wrong and made sure that she had respect for herself and wouldn't let any boy touch her or even consider sleeping with him until they were married. Or so I thought.

After a few months I could tell it was becoming serious between them; they were hardly ever apart. But after everything I'd been through, I certainly didn't want her getting married so young. It's the traveller way for girls to get married when they are still in their teens but I hoped that Sarah-Jane might travel or have a career before she settled down. My entire life had been dominated by my husband and I wanted something different for her. She knew I had dreams for her but Sarah-Jane had struggled at school and whenever I asked her what kind of job she'd like to do, she wasn't really interested.

Then one afternoon fairly soon after her seventeenth birthday I was taking some shopping out of the car boot when I noticed a pregnancy test, almost hidden in the corner.

'Where the hell did that come from?' I said.

'Maybe you picked it up by mistake,' Sarah-Jane said.

I put it in a kitchen cupboard, thinking a friend might need it one day. I certainly had no intention of ever needing it again myself. Then a few days after that I was mowing the lawn and found the empty box at the bottom of the garden underneath a tree. 'There's something strange going on here,' I thought. But honest to God it still never occurred to me for a second that my child might be pregnant.

A week later, Sarah-Jane, Jason and a few of their mates were round mine for something to eat. 'Let's open you a bottle of wine, shall we?' said Jason. I stared at him. Why would I be drinking wine on a Tuesday teatime – I never did. I'd just taken my first mouthful when he came right out with it. 'Me and Sarah-Jane want to marry.'

I spat the drink straight back in the glass. 'What?' I said. 'Why?'

'Erm, erm, erm . . . erm,' he went on, looking terrified.

'You're only babies yourselves,' I said. 'You can't get married yet. It's madness. If you're serious about each other why don't you get engaged then wait a couple of years and see if you still feel the same about marriage then.'

But whatever I said there was no budging them. They told me that Jason's parents wanted to go off travelling again soon so they wanted to be wed before they left. Still, like a total eedjit, I accepted what they said.

'I know this isn't what you wanted for me, Mum,' Sarah-Jane said to me that night. 'I know you didn't want me to marry until I was at least 30 but me and Jason aren't like you and Daddy. It's going to be OK.'

All I could do was pray that she was right about that. I could see how happy they were together and part of me wished I'd had that when I was their age. I'd fallen into marriage without ever really being in love.

'Well, you'll still have to ask her father,' I told Jason. No matter what I thought of Stevie, things still needed to be done properly and in the traveller culture a father's permission is required before a marriage can go ahead.

Stevie was dead set against the idea at first but they managed to talk him round. He didn't have any money for the wedding so I was going to have to pay for everything. Thankfully Jason's family and culture of travellers didn't believe in fortunes being paid for women, otherwise there is absolutely no way I would have been able to afford for her to get married. Even then, I was still worrying myself sick about how I was going to manage it on my wages.

He was no help at all and every time we discussed plans he was drunk and aggressive.

'You just think you're it dontcha because you've got a job and a house and a fancy TV,' he kept saying. 'Well don't you forget that the only thing you are is my wife.'

'I don't care what I am,' I yelled back. 'All I know is that if you've got nothing to contribute, I don't want to see you again until the wedding day.'

I had just six weeks to sort out the wedding and it became a total nightmare. Traveller weddings are always huge events and I was expecting at least 200 people to turn up. I just couldn't afford to have a wedding like some of those that go on nowadays in the traveller community. I've been to weddings of my friends' and cousins' children and the bride is wearing a dress the size of a tent that she can barely walk in, let alone breathe in. At one wedding, the dress had tiny diamonds sewn into the bodice and the poor wee girl getting married was wearing a crown like the Queen's. Over the past five years or so, families have been spending more and more money, just because they feel that's what they're supposed to do, but I don't agree with it. It's an important day but it seems disgusting to spend that much money on a dress and a glass carriage and arriving by helicopter or whatever. As I've discovered, there's a lot more to marriage than a big dress and a glass carriage.

No, Sarah-Jane's wedding was going to be a lot more low-key, although by settled people's standards it was still a huge event with a champagne reception, red carpet and 12 bridesmaids. Daddy sent me some money to help out and after that I was dependent on any other donations I was offered from family and friends. If you count all my aunties, uncles and cousins I have a huge family by most country people's standards. And in traveller culture, families are used to pitching in to help out with wedding costs if money is tight.

I'd suffered discrimination throughout my life for being a traveller, but the worst I've ever known was when I came to book that wedding reception.

At the first hotel I made a booking over the phone but when I turned up and they heard my accent and made the connection with my name, McKinley, which is a known traveller name, they suddenly realised they'd double-booked and they couldn't possibly let the other people down. I knew it was a lie but what could I say? It happens to travellers trying to arrange any sort of family gathering, all the time. Hotel and restaurant owners are always worried that with the number of people that attend these events it'll end in trouble. And yes, sometimes there are fights, but most times it is all perfectly pleasant. And besides, you get fights at country people's weddings too.

The second hotel I found seemed much more promising. I went to look around and the manageress talked me through the menu, where the photographs would be taken and where the DJ would be positioned. It was all just grand. And then I started giving her the names of the people who'd be sitting at the top table: O'Hara, McKinley, Walsh. As I reeled them off she was staring at me and I knew then it was all over.

'And would you be members of the travelling community perhaps?' she said, all snooty.

'We are, that's right,' I replied. There seemed no point in hiding it now.

'OK, well we'll be back in touch with you soon about the booking,' she said.

'No, you won't be back to me,' I said, turning to walk away with tears stinging in my eyes. 'I can guarantee that you won't.'

And of course I never heard from her again.

Time was running out and I was becoming increasingly desperate to find somewhere willing to host a traveller wedding reception. On top of that I was still working every day and I was supposed to be preparing for an English exam too. I was going up the walls with worry. I tried at least half a dozen other places but it was the same story at each of them. I had just one left on my list to visit. The manageress was showing me around the banqueting suite when she came out with the question I'd been dreading.

'Er, excuse me, Mrs McKinley,' she said. 'But are you a traveller?'

'Please don't tell me, "No",' I said. 'Please don't say, "No". It's my eldest child's wedding and I've got to find a place. There'll be no trouble. I promise.'

The manageress went into a long story about how they'd had a traveller wedding once before and it ended up with furniture getting smashed and a chandelier being shattered.

'But not all travellers are the same,' I tried desperately to explain. 'It's the same as with settled people like you, you're not all the same.'

She could see I had a point and she must surely have seen how desperate I was.

'OK,' she said. 'But I'll need a big deposit and please don't make me regret this.'

'Oh, I won't,' I said. I could have kissed her right there and then.

I wonder if she got in trouble with her boss for agreeing to the reception though, because the next time I saw her she was far more frosty. She doubled the amount she wanted for the deposit to £2,000 and then on the eve of the wedding announced she wanted the entire payment in cash up front before a single guest was allowed on the premises.

On the day itself, things got worse when Jason and his best man were pulled over in their car twice on the way to the church.

'We've not done anything, Sir,' Jason told the police officers. 'I'm on my way to get married.'

The second time, they thought he was making it all up and was giving them false names so in the end they followed him to the church to make sure he was telling the truth. It didn't bode well, having the groom arrive with a police escort! Once the police were content that Jason really was who he said he was they drove off and let us be.

None of that mattered in the end, though. The service was beautiful and when Sarah-Jane walked down the aisle in her chiffon dress with diamante bodice she looked incredible, like a real princess. Me and Stevie kept our distance from each other and he was under strict orders from his family not to cause trouble. Mammy was too poorly to be there but Daddy came and it was great to spend time with him. The whole day was lovely. It was certainly a very different wedding to my register office do all those years ago. I just hoped Sarah-Jane's marriage would be very different to mine too.

21

Goodbye Stevie

I walked into the council chamber physically shaking with nerves. 'What on earth am I doing here?' I asked myself.

I was at a meeting of the city council for a discussion about travellers' conditions at sites in the area. All around me were men and women with sharp accents and smart suits. They'd probably spent years working as doctors and lawyers. Most of them would have been to university and they probably now lived in those big houses with the white gates on the outskirts of the city.

And here was me sitting next to them, the girl born on a pavement.

It was my first big meeting as a member of the local travellers' support group. Mick, the manager at the site where we had been living had first introduced me to the group. He knew I was getting on with my reading and writing and had enjoyed teaching the other travellers at night classes. 'Come on, Rosie,' he said. 'You're just the person we're looking for. You can talk plainly and openly with the travellers then represent their thoughts and concerns to the bigwigs on the council.'

It sounded scary but I agreed anyway and soon I was attending meetings once a month. Even after we moved into our house I carried on attending the groups. I wasn't actually living in a trailer any more, but I was still a traveller.

That is my culture, just as much as other people's culture is Jewish or Afro-Caribbean or whatever it may be.

At each meeting a group of us travellers would discuss any new issues affecting our community. The topics ranged from discrimination, medical care and site cleanliness, to how to ensure the kids kept up their education and were able to play safely. At first a lot of the discussions went way over my head and I didn't like the formal meetings and their big posh words. I didn't understand what a proposal was or what local government funding really meant. But gradually I picked things up. And when they were talking about things I really couldn't grasp, I'd go home and try to unpick the mystery with the help of my dictionary.

I loved it. The best thing was contributing something to the conversation and feeling that other people were listening. Travellers from all over Bristol and the surrounding area were represented on the committee and I was responsible for making sure their voices were presented accurately at meetings of the city and local councils. I took the role seriously and would report back what had been discussed to other travellers and gather their comments for the next meeting.

From there I found myself being asked to join other committees and working groups. I was nominated to a committee for ethnic minorities living in Bristol. Then there was another for kids from disadvantaged backgrounds and another to encourage low-income families to eat more healthily and another on how to ensure a fair access to education for everyone. Soon I was at meetings three or four nights a week. Friends would help out with babysitting and I'd catch up with the mountains of paperwork to be read when the kids were at school during the day. Sometimes I'd be up until the early hours if there was a big proposal document to read or if we were trying to put together a document to bid for lottery or government funding for an important new project.

At the beginning I'd go to meetings and we would discuss the leaflets to be distributed among travellers to inform them about a new project or initiative. 'Well, that's no good,' I finally plucked up the courage to say. 'A traveller won't respond to that kind of language – this is how you need to say it.' Then I picked up a pen and rewrote the whole leaflet. The other committee members were delighted. Finally they had someone who could really communicate with travellers but who was interested in working with settled people to make their conditions better.

It was time-consuming and challenging but with my dictionary at my side I ploughed through endless documents and typed out reports and recommendations that would be delivered to the most important people on the city council. And each time one of the committees or working groups had a success and won funding for a project that helped travellers or introduced new rules that made life fairer for the travelling community, then I knew the hard work was worthwhile.

One of the reasons I got so involved with all the committees and meetings was that I found it too quiet at home without Sarah-Jane around. After the wedding she had immediately gone over to Ireland to travel with Jason's family. I missed her desperately.

She would phone home several times a week and I could tell she was enjoying being married.

'You enjoy yourselves,' I said to her on the phone one

day. 'But don't you two be thinking about kids for a few years yet. See a bit of the world first.'

'Yeah, yeah, yeah,' she replied.

'Sarah-Jane, listen to me,' I said. 'You're only a child yourself, don't be thinking about having a baby.' It went very quiet at the other end of the phone but I didn't think anything more of it.

A couple of days later, about three weeks after the wedding, Sarah-Jane called again. She was clearly very nervous. 'I've got something to tell you,' she said.

'Oh yes?' I replied, immediately concerned.

'I'm pregnant,' she said.

'Jeez, that was quick!' I replied. I couldn't help but feel disappointed that her life was now going to revolve around caring for her husband and child, just as mine had done. But I tried to sound enthusiastic. Her husband was a good man and they were clearly very happy together.

By my calculations the due date was going to be May but Sarah-Jane wanted me to go over to Ireland a couple of months before to help her prepare for the baby. When I arrived it was March and I thought she looked enormous if she still had eight weeks to go. I spent a few days helping her out then went home, intending to return when the baby was born. But I'd barely stepped in the door and put the kettle on when I picked up a message from Jason on the answer-machine. 'The baby is coming early,' he was saying frantically. 'You've got to come back.'

My suitcase had split while I was in Ireland and Jason had lent me one of theirs so I quickly pulled my dirty clothes out and started packing some clean ones. But it was then I noticed some letters that had clearly been left in the case by mistake. When I pulled them out I couldn't help noticing that one was from the hospital and was addressed to Sarah-Jane. It was the results from an earlier scan and at the bottom it gave the baby's due date as March 22 – which was the previous day. Finally everything fell into place. The mystery pregnancy test packet, the rushed wedding and then the 'premature' baby. I couldn't believe I hadn't guessed a thing. That is how naïve I could still be about things like sex outside of marriage! Even now, when un-married teenage girls get pregnant all the time, it never entered my mind that it would happen to my daughter.

I rang Jason's mobile phone.

'Oh Rosie, you've got to come,' he said. 'The baby's coming early.'

'It's not though, is it Jason?' I said. 'The baby is coming bang on time. Listen, it's all fine, but tell me the truth.'

There was a silence on the other end of the phone that seemed to go on for an hour and a half. 'Well. Yes,' he said finally.

'OK, I'll be there as soon as I can,' I replied. Obviously I was disappointed that Sarah-Jane hadn't confided in me but by then all that mattered was that my little girl and the baby were OK. I just wanted to be there for her.

I couldn't get a flight back to Ireland until the following morning so all that night I was ringing Jason every 20 minutes for an update. In between times I sat and prayed that Sarah-Jane and her baby would be well. When Lila Rosie was born, weighing 7lb 3oz, in the early hours of the morning, I was the proudest granny in the world.

I took all the kids over to see their new niece and we had a wonderful time all together. The only sadness for Sarah-Jane was that her Daddy didn't visit his first grandchild. She rang him and he said he'd come over but he was clearly drinking again.

We arranged a christening and we waited and waited, hoping Stevie would come. He may not have been a brilliant husband or father but he was Lila's grand-dadddy and Sarah-Jane still idolised him.

In the end we decided we'd have to go ahead without Stevie. We were all standing at the font at the front of the church when the door opened at the other end of the aisle. Me and Sarah-Jane looked back, thinking it might be Stevie. There was a bright ray of sunlight coming in the door against which there appeared to be a shadow of a tall, broad man with wild, shaggy hair. It was the exact silhouette of Stevie. But when I looked again, the shadow had gone and the door had blown shut. An optical illusion, I thought to myself. We went on with the christening and had a few drinks afterwards to celebrate. It was a beautiful day but at the end Sarah-Jane cried a few tears because her daddy hadn't been there to see it.

Four days later I went home. I'd only been in the house half an hour when the phone rang. It was Sarah-Jane. 'Mammy,' she said. 'Daddy's dead.'

He'd died two days before the christening. I'll be convinced for evermore that the shadow at the door of the church was Stevie's spirit coming to say goodbye to his children and the granddaughter he'd never met. And to me too, I suppose. Whatever our differences had been over the years, he was still my husband. I felt like part of me had been ripped away.

I hate the idea that Stevie was on his own when he died. Alone in a scruffy, dirty, one-bedroom flat with barely a single possession apart from one picture of his family from a day trip to the beach when the kids were little.

Apparently he'd been out the previous night drinking, and partying during the day with a rough crowd he was hanging around with back in Manchester. He'd been celebrating becoming a grandfather, which somehow made it particularly tragic. He was last seen on his way back to his flat in the early hours of the morning. But soon after he got home he had a massive heart attack and died.

His body was only found three days later when one of his mates called round to see why he hadn't been out for a few nights.

All the kids were devastated but Sarah-Jane took it worse. She'd known her daddy in the years before he was really drinking heavily and I guess she had a bigger bank of memories of the things they'd done together. 'My Sarah-Jane,' he'd call her and she really was.

For me, it was the strangest time. Whatever had happened between us, he was still the father of my children and for good or bad our lives had been intertwined for more than 20 years. I felt totally shocked and quite tearful. But at the same time I also felt a strange sensation of being free for the first time in my adult life. For years I'd lived my life dominated by Stevie, either waiting for him to turn up after one of his disappearing acts, or later on, waiting for him to find us each time we managed to escape from him.

Now it was over. I was never going to see him again.

Sarah-Jane and I arranged to meet in Manchester to get his body released from the mortuary and to bring him down to Cornwall where he could be buried near his family. Bridget came to support us and I was grateful for that. I took the kids with me. It was the right thing to do to go to fetch their Daddy and to bring him back to be buried with dignity and respect. But we were travelling for 12 hours back and forward to Manchester and after it the kids were exhausted and really upset.

On the day of the funeral we all sat at the front of the church as they brought in Stevie's coffin with a huge framed photograph of him on top of it. He looked just as handsome as when I'd first met him, before the drink and partying and bad tempers had shaded the way I saw him.

He'd joked with me years before that when he died he'd send me a message to let me know if he was in heaven or hell. So when they laid the coffin down and all the lights in the church flickered, I knew that was the message. It wasn't exactly clear whether it meant heaven or hell though! I like to think he is in heaven, God rest his soul.

When we went to the grave, Finn wanted to shake some earth onto the coffin like all the other men but he was still very slight for a 14-year-old and he could barely lift the shovel. But he wouldn't let that stop him. He wanted to do it for his daddy. It broke my heart.

The kids were tired and exhausted after the funeral – it had been a really traumatic time for them. They hadn't eaten properly for days so Bridget and I decided to take them to a nearby pub that did bar meals. We went in and sat in the corner quietly. Everyone was very subdued. My eyes were puffy from crying and my head was pounding.

I got the kids a bowl of soup each but they could barely eat it and I had to spoon feed Grace. Afterwards I went to the bar and ordered two coffees and a small beer for myself.

'I'm not serving you drink,' the barman said.

'I'm sorry?' I replied, feeling a bit confused.

'I've served you food but I'll not be serving drink,' he said.

I felt like I'd been kicked in the stomach.

'I've just buried my husband,' I said, my voice starting to choke. 'Those kiddies have just buried their daddy. Now will you please serve me some drinks.'

All around the bar other people were drinking and carrying on perfectly normally.

The barman looked straight through me.

'Is this because we're travellers?' I said.

'I'll give you no reason,' he replied. 'I've sold you some food but there'll be no drinks.'

I was mortified that it had happened in front of the children and they'd been made to feel second rate on the day of their father's funeral. I gathered them together and we walked out with as much dignity as we could manage. I was sure he'd been told there had been a traveller funeral in the nearby church and thinking there would be trouble, he was refusing to serve us. It was so wrong and so unfair. It happens all the time that travellers get turned away from restaurants and pubs after funerals because country people always expect the worst from us.

I was devastated but also seething angry. 'This doesn't end here,' I vowed to Bridget as we got in the car.

And it didn't. I had spent the last few months working with the council authorities to end this sort of discrimination. I knew a lot more about the law and I felt far more confident than I had ever done before. That night I did some research on the internet and it was clear that what the pub barman had done wasn't just unkind, it was also illegal.

Under the equalities legislation, a person cannot be barred from somewhere on the basis of their race or cultural background. I immediately emailed the address for the head office of the equalities commission with my story.

Next morning I went into town and found a solicitor. 'I want to bring action against the pub,' I said. 'This isn't about winning money from them. It's about showing people they can't keep discriminating against us just because we're travellers. We've got to prove that we're not all the way the newspapers say we are. That stuff is just wrong.'

Over the next few months, letters went backwards and forwards between our lawyers as each side tried to prove and disprove exactly what happened that day. Finally after almost a year, my case went to trial and was accepted by a judge. I only received a tiny pay-out but my costs were paid by the pub and most importantly for me, I'd won the case for travellers everywhere.

For months after Stevie's death I walked around in a daze. Sarah-Jane was my best friend as well as my daughter but she was hundreds of miles away in Ireland. I felt lonely and fed-up. I was still working at the nursing home and for years I had loved it, but then three of the residents who I'd been close to all died, one after the other. I was at a low ebb already and it really hit me. I couldn't face any more sadness so I gave up the job.

I threw myself into the work with the traveller groups and with the kids to look after too I was always busy, busy, busy. But deep down, I was quite unhappy. I would never have admitted it, but something was missing.

Traditionally, a good traveller wife would remain loyal to her husband even after his death and would never remarry.

Some traveller women wear nothing but mourning black for
two or three years after their bereavement. Me and Stevie had
barely lived together for years but I still felt I had to mourn
him properly and it never entered my head to look for another
man. So I just got on with things and tried to push the feelings
of loneliness and sadness as deep inside me as I could.

It was almost a year after Stevie died that I went out for
the first time with some friends into town for a drink one
Friday night. A couple of fellas came up and started talking
to us. One of them introduced himself as Terry and was
asking me loads of questions and seemed really interested
in me. I thought it all seemed a bit strange that he was so
keen but he was funny and made me laugh. I liked him. At
the end of the evening, Terry leaned across and said,
'Would you give me your telephone number please?'

I hesitated for a second. There was never going to be a
perfect moment to drop this into conversation, so it might
as well be now. 'I'm a traveller,' I said.

'So?' came his reply. 'Now, about that number . . .'

I wrote it down for him and I was still on my way home
when he started texting me. Then we started talking via
instant messaging online. Within days we knew all about
each other but I still wasn't sure about the whole idea of
going out with him on a date.

He asked me again and again to go out for dinner with
him but I kept coming up with excuses. In the end I agreed
and we met three or four times for meals or walks or trips
to the cinema. But he never tried to kiss me or make a move.
I'd told him all about Stevie so he knew I didn't want to
rush into a new relationship. And I was nervous about
getting into anything serious with him because I was still

recently a widow and I'd be ostracised in the traveller community for it. Particularly as he was a country man. At the same time, I didn't half fancy him! I was still a traveller girl through and through, though, and I'd have died rather than make the first move.

Despite all my worries, I was enjoying myself. It was a far more relaxed relationship than I would have had with a traveller. In traveller relationships, I feel the girl is almost expected to play a role and has to become the type of partner the fella has in mind. With Terry, I could be myself – and he seemed to like it!

After a month we finally kissed. I knew already that I was in love with him. But that brought a lorry-load of problems with it. What if a traveller saw me with him? What would I tell the kids? What would his family think? I decided the best policy at first was to keep our relationship top secret. I wouldn't go out anywhere locally with him in case we were seen together.

'Will you come away with me for the weekend?' he asked one evening.

'I will not,' I replied. I still had a very strict moral code about things like sex outside of marriage. But then I spent the next few days thinking about what I'd said and asked myself all sorts of questions I'd never considered before. 'Why was sex outside of marriage wrong if I loved the man?' and, 'Who was I worried about offending by dating a country man?' and, 'Would those people worry about offending me?'

When Terry rang back that evening, I said, 'About that weekend. I'll come.'

We had a beautiful, relaxing time just the two of us. I was truly happy.

Terry had one son from his first marriage and he wanted me to meet him. I wanted him to meet my children too but I was terrified about how they would react, thinking they'd be angry and say I shouldn't have done it with their daddy just dead.

We were just about to set up the meeting when things took a very dramatic turn. My period was late. And I was pregnant.

I couldn't believe it. The last thing I'd had in mind for my future was to become a mother again. Because Terry and I hadn't been together that long I just hadn't got round to going on the Pill. I honestly never thought I would fall pregnant that quickly. You'd think I'd have learnt my lesson by then at just how quickly I could fall but I hadn't.

Now I faced having to tell the children that not only had I got a new boyfriend, they were about to have a new brother or sister too!

But first I had to break the news to Terry. We'd only been together four months but the moment I told him he broke into a broad smile. 'It's fantastic,' he said. 'It's all going to be great.'

I was so relieved I felt like crying.

Now it was my turn to explain to Sarah-Jane about getting pregnant. I thought she'd go mad. 'Mammy, you deserve it,' she said. 'You've done enough to look after other people, look after yourself for a change.'

The other children were just as excited and within a few weeks Terry moved into our house and it was like he'd always been there. His son came to visit at weekends and the kids all got on great together. Against an awful lot of odds, things seemed to be working out.

22

Always a Gypsy Girl

Sometimes, when I'm sitting with Terry and the kids of an evening and we're talking about what we've been up to that day, I almost think I can smell woodsmoke.

I'm transported back to my evenings as a child when everyone sat around the fire chatting and laughing about their day until the air grew cold and the night was silent.

It's all so different now though. Instead of a wood fire outside a two-roomed trailer and no running water, I'm living in the comfortable, three-bedroom semi-detached house that Terry and I have been able to buy together. We've got a well-tended garden that looks over countryside at the back and a nice car parked on the front drive.

I still miss the old days though, I really do. I don't think I could go back to living in a trailer permanently, I've become spoiled by central heating and hot showers and a dishwasher. But I drive everyone mad every month or so by moving all the furniture around or totally redecorating. And wherever I live, I will always be a traveller.

It wasn't easy when word got out that I was seeing a country man and had fallen pregnant by him. Even now, some of the traveller women that I used to call friends still won't speak to me. It doesn't affect my work with travellers in and around Bristol though because those most offended are family and friends of Stevie, down in Cornwall. While

I remained a widow I was regarded as the best wife and mammy in the world. But once I stepped out and tried to grab a bit of happiness for myself, then they didn't want to know me.

Not long after I started seeing Terry, I went to a relative's wedding and two women came up and called me a whore to my face. 'Your husband was barely dead and you went with another man,' one of the women spat at me.

I was mortified but what could I do? She wasn't interested in hearing the truth about the years of unhappiness and loneliness I'd had before finally finding a bit of peace. There was no point in explaining because I knew that in many travellers' minds I'd broken the rules. It seems I was expected to be not just 'a wife for life' but a wife in death too.

I can understand why some travellers are unhappy about traveller women settling down with a country man or moving into a house. They fear that each time this happens the culture becomes a little more diluted and the old ways get more forgotten. But I feel strongly that being a traveller is who I am, it's not about where I live. It's like being Jewish or Afro-Caribbean – it doesn't matter where you live, it is who you are.

My children live in a house but they have been brought up as travellers. I've taught the girls to respect themselves and all the children not to get involved with drugs. They've learnt to be respectful of their elders and they also know some of our ancient traveller language and understand how it has survived for centuries.

I hope they remain happy to be part of that culture but I know that Grace and Finn have tried to keep it quiet at school. When Grace was 14, I realised one day from something that she said that she hadn't told any of her friends she was a traveller. I spoke to her teacher about it. There is such an emphasis on diversity in schools now and I wanted her to feel comfortable about her background in school, as well as at home. I got a brilliant response from the teacher, who was really helpful.

A couple of days later the teacher was getting the kids to talk about their backgrounds and some Asian, Afro-Caribbean and Eastern European kids started talking about their families.

'And is there anyone here who is from the travelling culture?' the teacher said afterwards.

Grace completely blanked the question.

'No?' said the teacher. 'Anyone at all?'

Grace still wouldn't admit to it. I think that's sad and we've talked about it at home. I know it is because she is worried about the bullying and name-calling that still goes on towards traveller kids even now, just as much as when I was at school. But I don't want my kids to have to change who they are – I want society to change and to be more tolerant of everyone in it.

Discrimination against travellers remains a big problem and a lot of the work I do on traveller committees across the South West of England is focused on trying to bring that to an end. We have also done a lot of work on the medical conditions and life expectancy of travellers. We did a survey of thousands of travellers and the results made for desperate reading. Travellers are still far more prone to depression and alcoholism than settled people and the number of suicides is way above the national average. It is a tough life with the exposure to the weather, the lack of access to education and the discrimination, and a lot of travellers struggle to cope with that. For years the rules were so clear cut in the traveller world and everyone knew where they stood. But now the lines are far more blurred and that has made it hard for people to work out where they fit, both in their own culture and in their wider society. I'm sure that has added to the cases of depression that the community has had and the alcohol addiction which has been a result of it. And to make things worse, when travellers do suffer from depression it is rarely spotted and treated properly because few are even registered with a GP. So when they do get into difficulties they have nowhere to turn.

There has also been an increase in the use of drugs in the traveller community. It used to be that travellers would never touch drugs but now everywhere you go there's cocaine, heroin, speed, marijuana, anything you want. Even quite young kids are getting into drugs now.

Poor education also remains a big problem for travellers. The majority of people in the community still can't read or write and we are still getting kids slipping through the schooling net by being moved from pillar to post throughout their childhood. Some of these problems stem from decades of discrimination but undoubtedly some of them are due to travellers refusing to engage or get involved with settled society. There is still a huge feeling of distrust towards country people and that prevents travellers from doing things like registering with doctors, dentists, opticians and schools.

A lot of the groups I've been involved with have worked

on projects to encourage interaction between settled and traveller kids through sport and craft activities. But a lot of traveller families don't want their children to be involved in that sort of thing. They don't want to break down the barriers that separate the communities because they think they're better off keeping as far away from country people as possible. The fear of being rejected and harassed is still very strong.

And that mutual lack of trust can feel impossible to break down because the reality is that travellers are still discriminated against every single day. Most travellers will be well used to hearing the insults, 'Gypo' or 'Pikey', flung at them when they're out. They'll also be wrongly accused of stealing and fighting, just because that is the reputation we have. And they'll be banned from bars and restaurants for no other reason than their background.

I think a lot of settled people don't understand how bad the discrimination is. In this country we have got used to expecting that people will be treated equally and people find it hard to believe that there are still pockets of society where that is not the case. If a black man walked into a bar and the manager refused to serve him there would be a national outcry. And rightly so. But that sort of thing is happening to travellers somewhere in the country every single day of the week.

Everything you read about travellers in the newspapers is bad. Bad, bad, bad. We're either camping on people's back lawns, or nicking things or fighting. But there is so much crime in every town caused by settled people, which never gets reported in the same way.

I think the only way we'll ever end the discrimination is

by talking to settled people about our culture and hoping that they start to see us as individuals. I now do talks to youth groups, schools, councillors and health trusts about travellers and the different cultures within our community. I tell them the facts about how travellers live, the way they think about issues and the differences in beliefs and practices within the community.

I feel going into schools is the most important part of what I do. I had such a miserable time at school, being endlessly bullied by the settled kids or sidelined by the teachers, and I always hope that if one of my talks stops just one traveller kid from getting bullied then it will have been worthwhile.

I'm still very strict on the kids about doing their homework and making sure they study hard at school. There's no TV or playing out with their friends until it has all been finished. And while they have to keep their bedrooms tidy and clear the table after dinner, I never make them do the amount of housework me and Bridget had to do as kids. Back then girls were helping to run the home from a really early age. But I wouldn't do that to my children. I think they should be learning or playing rather than polishing horse brasses or mopping floors. There's plenty enough time for cleaning when they're older. And although Sarah-Jane married young and has been very happy, I don't really want that for my other kids. If you marry as a teenager you're married for an awful long time. And what is the rush? I want my children to be children, they'll be adults for long enough in the future.

Thank goodness all the children have done OK at school. Finn passed seven GCSEs and is staying on at school to take a couple of A levels and hopes to one day work in computing. When he received his exam results I was so proud of him. To think a few years ago I could barely read and write and now my son has all these qualifications.

Grace is also doing well and has made lots of good friends. She is still reluctant to tell people about her traveller background but I think that might be because as a teenage girl she has a natural desire to just be like everyone else in her class. I'm hopeful that when she gets a bit older then she will be far more open about her culture.

Tyrone has a good job working locally as a plumber and has a steady girlfriend with whom he is very happy. I know he still misses his daddy and sometimes we talk about the good times we did all have together in the past.

Sarah-Jane is living in Ireland and now has two children of her own. They are growing up so quickly so I make sure I travel over to see them whenever I can.

My brother Danny still lives with us as he will always need to be looked after because of his learning difficulties but he attends a special college during term time. My brother Pauly lives up in Manchester near our daddy and is working as a builder. We speak on the phone every week.

Tina and Maria both married traveller boys but are living in houses now, as is Bridget. The other boys, Kevin, Sean and Tommy have all married really nice women too and have remained living in trailers, although they are fairly permanently based around the Manchester area. We speak on the phone regularly and see each other at family parties, weddings and funerals but it is hard to see them all more frequently than that.

Ol'Mammy died eight years ago after suffering from cancer for a couple of years. Mammy followed her two years ago. She drank herself to death. We tried everything we could to help her but if someone doesn't want to save herself then there's very little you can do. I think both women never really got over Ol'Daddy dying and in many ways I think they were both probably relieved to be going to be with him again.

I'm now pretty convinced that Mammy must have had a nervous breakdown after her daddy died, she found out about her husband's affair and then Danny was born so poorly, all in such a short space of time. But because she didn't get the medical treatment she needed at the time, she turned to drink, which developed into an addiction that she couldn't kick. Now when I look back at the few photos I have from my childhood, of us kids with her and Daddy, it looks like a different lifetime. We're laughing away with big fat smiles on our faces, with no idea how hard the future was going to be.

Daddy is still living with Shirley and they are happy together. Despite the age gap and all my concerns, they've been together more than 20 years now.

I was very worried how Daddy would react when I told him I was pregnant by Terry, especially as they hadn't even met at that point. But he was great about it. 'You deserve a bit of happiness,' he said straight away.

Sometimes I wonder if I was too hard on him when he broke the traveller rules and fell in love with another woman. I still find it upsetting that he cheated on Mammy but as I've got older I've learnt it isn't always possible to live life by rules, particularly if you want to be happy. I certainly played by the rules for so many years and it didn't bring me much happiness. But by meeting and moving in with Terry I broke every rule in the book and felt content in myself for the first time in my life.

Terry and I talk all the time about anything and everything. We are equals in everything we do. We both want the same things in life: to have a nice home, well-behaved kids and peace. He doesn't drink much and when we do go out and have a few he is a jolly drunk, never violent or aggressive.

In January 2010 I gave birth to our daughter. She has Terry's fair complexion and brilliant blue eyes. We called her Hope, because she has given all of us hope for an amazing new future together. Terry even changes her nappies, so I don't need any better proof than that, that I've met the perfect man!

I still spend a lot of time working on support groups and committees to help travellers and often have to put together reports that will be read by hundreds of people. It seems incredible that I've been given the chance to do this when as a child I only ever owned one book, *James and the Giant Peach*. And then Mammy threw that on the fire. Now there are dozens of books in our house and I love learning new things.

It has been a slow process but now when I look at other people around the table in the meetings I attend, I can think, 'I'm as good as you.' Maybe that sounds big-headed but what I mean is that I grew up thinking those kind of people were way more important than me. But now I realise no one is more important than anyone else, we're just different. Travellers aren't any worse or any better than settled people, they just live their lives differently. And that is what I hope people will understand more and more in the future.

Things are certainly changing in the traveller community. Much of that change is positive but some of it I do find worrying. The position of women is a good example. Traveller women have always taken great pride in their appearance. Before Mammy started drinking she would spend a fortune making sure she looked amazing with her expensive clothes and bulging make-up bag. But now there is a craze for women to spend vast amounts of money on plastic surgery. They're having their lips, noses, boobs, bellies, arses, anything at all done then wearing more and more revealing outfits so everyone can see them. Traveller girls are also drinking alcohol before they are married in a way they never would before. So with all the revealing clothes and binge drinking, some of the single traveller girls are going astray, although in general, traveller girls do still remain virgins until they are married.

I'm glad that traveller girls are getting more independence, of course, and going out with their friends and getting jobs, as they were never allowed to do before. But it does make me sad that these girls are expressing that independence by getting blasted on Bacardi Breezers!

I think, in many ways it is far more difficult to be a traveller now than when I was a child. It is getting harder and harder for travellers to protect their culture. In part that's a consequence of some of the other, more positive changes: with more contact between travellers and settled people, a lot of the things that have happened in the settled world over the past twenty years are now affecting us too, but with devastating consequences. Things like binge drinking, drugs, lack of respect for elders and relationship break-ups are all problems that were unknown when I was a child.

There is also a lack of good sites for travellers. The government and local councils closed down a lot of sites and there are no temporary sites anywhere any more. When I was a kid you could park up on a verge or in a car park and stay there for a couple of weeks with no trouble at all. But then councils started blocking up entrances and building up verges to make it harder and harder for us to have anywhere to stop. They preferred to have us all penned into these massive sites away from towns, which they could then forget about. There is a huge amount of work going on among voluntary groups and some local authorities to encourage travellers to mix with the rest of society but you can't get away from the reality that a lot of people in power want travellers put somewhere where they're not seen or heard.

I do believe a lot of people are working very hard to make things better for travellers and to end discrimination against them, but it is going to be a slow process. We are starting from a very very tough place. 92 per cent of travellers have no GCSEs and only a terrifyingly small 10 per cent of travellers live beyond 40 years of age. Only 1 per cent live beyond 60. There has been discrimination against travellers for hundreds of years and it is going to take a long time for that to be turned around but I think gradually it will be. All I want is for people to realise that in most ways, travellers are no different to anyone else; all they want is to live in peace and to be able to give their kids a good life in the culture within which they've lived for generations.

As for me, as well as my voluntary work on behalf of

travellers, I've now passed GCSEs in English, History and Maths and I'm hoping to train to be a nurse. I've got Terry, my beautiful new baby, all my other children, my grand-children and brothers and sisters and a future that I am truly looking forward to.

I feel very fortunate to have had the life I've had. I'm proud to be a traveller and for everything that my culture has given me. But most of all, I'm grateful for how being a traveller has taught me that home isn't just a trailer or four walls and a roof, home is the people that you love.